Noodles

Classical Chinese Cooking 精華篇

作　　　者　　林麗華
出　版　者　　純青出版社有限公司
　　　　　　　台北市松江路125號4樓
　　　　　　　郵政劃撥：12106299
　　　　　　　電話：(02)2508-4331、2507-4902
　　　　　　　網址：www.weichuan.org.tw
　　　　　　　E-mail：we122179@ms13.hinet.net
著作財產權人　財團法人味全文化教育基金會
版 權 所 有　局版台業字第3884號
　　　　　　　中華民國83年1月初版發行
　　　　　　　中華民國88年12月三版發行
印　　　刷　　合同美術印刷廠股份有限公司
定　　　價　　新台幣貳佰捌拾元整

Author　　　　Lee　Hwa　Lin
Publisher　　　Chin Chin Publishing Co., Ltd.
　　　　　　　4th fl., 125, Sung Chiang Rd.,
　　　　　　　Taipei, Taiwan, R.O.C.
　　　　　　　Tel:(02)2508-4331・2507-4902
Distributor　　Wei-Chuan Publishing
　　　　　　　1455 Monterey Pass Rd., #110
　　　　　　　Monterey Park, CA91754, U.S.A.
　　　　　　　Tel :(323)2613880・2613878
　　　　　　　Fax:(323)2613299
Printer　　　　Ho Tong Art Printing Factory Co., Ltd.
　　　　　　　Printed in Taiwan, R.O.C.
Copyright　Holder　Copyright ©1990
　　　　　　　By Wei-Chuan Cultural-Educational Foundation
　　　　　　　First Printing, Jan., 1994
　　　　　　　Third Printing, Dec., 1999
　　　　　　　ISBN 0-941676-42-0

序

麵食可以待客嗎？只要擁有這本「精華篇」食譜，一道道色香俱全的麵點，將使餐桌上水乳交融、賓主盡歡。

中國地大物博，各種麵食都具有地方特色，而這本精華篇麵食食譜裡，集結了多種不同麵條的做法，無論炒麵、燴麵、涼拌麵或湯麵，都可成為宴席菜的佳餚，使人食指大動。

有鑑於此，味全文教基金會以一年多的時間，蒐尋中國各省各具風味的麵食，經悉心整理，將百餘道佳餚，規劃成「家常篇」與「精華篇」兩部分，分別編纂成兩本食譜。

「家常篇」首重小吃實用，做法簡單，材料俯拾可得，是現代家庭的烹調良方；「精華篇」則重豪華，以較精緻的素材調理出色彩豐富，美味可口的待客佳餚。

綜合兩本食譜，即可掌握中國麵食文化的精髓。

FOREWORD

Can a noodle dish be served as a main entree? With this book, Classical Chinese Cooking:Noodles, wide varieties of gourmet noodle dishes befitting all occassions can elegantly grace your dinner table bringing enjoyment to all palates.

Chinese noodle dishes are rich with the regional flavors of a vast land abundant in natural resources . This cookbook provides many methods for making and cooking a variety of noodle dishes .Whether noodles are fried, used in soups, cooked with sauces, or mixed , they can be served as an attractive and appetizing entree.

The Wei-Chuan Cultural-Education Foundation has devoted more than a year of research and effort gathering hundreds of regional noodle dishes. These recipes have been divided into two volumes--Chinese Home Cooking:Noodle and Classical Chinese Cooking: Noodles.

While the book Chinese Home Cooking: Noodles emphasizes practical and simple methods with materials that are easy to obtain and suit the basic needs of a modern family,Classical Chinese Cooking : Noodles offers recipes for appealing party dishes using fine materials and ingredients.

These two unique noodle cookbooks truly offer the essence of Chinese noodle cooking.

Lee Hwa Lin

目 錄

麵體製作 · *Methods of Noodle Making*

雞蛋麵 ....Egg Noodle **7**
菠菜麵 ....Spinach Noodle **8**
麵片 ....Noodle Pieces **9**
刀切麵 ....Handmade Noodle **9**
刀削麵 ....Shaved Noodle **10**
貓耳朵 ....Cat's Ears **10**

麵的煮法 · *Guide to Noodle Cooking Methods*

冷水煮麵 ....Boil Noodle **11**
油麵煮法 ....Boil Yellow Noodle **12**
麵線煮法 ....Boil Noodle String **12**
炸麵 ....Deep Fried Noodle **13**
伊麵 ....E-Fu Noodle **13**
兩面黃 ....Noodle Pancake **13**

材料的前處理 · *Preparation of Special Food Materials*

花枝的處理 ....Squid **14**
海參的發法 ....Dried Sea Cucumber **14**
蝦仁清洗方法 ....Shrimp **15**
海哲皮的處理 ....Jelly Fish **15**
牛筋的處理 ....Beef Tendon **15**
薑泥和薑汁的製作 ....Ginger Paste and Ginger Juice **16**
蒜泥的製作 ....Garlic Paste **16**
銀芽 ....Bean Sprout **16**
筍的處理 ....Bamboo Shoot **16**
蔥段的切法 ....Green Onion Sections **17**
洋菇的處理 ....Mushroom **17**
番茄的處理 ....Tomato **17**

烹調的方法 · *Guide to Cooking Terms*

上湯的製作 ....Consommé **18**
高湯的製作 ....Stock **18**
煮出汁的製作 ....Seaweed Stock **19**
川燙 ....Parboil **19**
過油 ....Hot Oil Soaking **19**

各種麵體的説明與換算 .... *General Information on Noodle Weight Equivalent Chart* **20**

湯麵 · *Soup Noodle*

斑球伊麵 ....Fish Fillet Soup E-Fu Noodle **22**
銀魚湯麵 ....Silver Fish Soup Noodle **24**

Contents

黃魚煨麵 ....Yellow Fish Braised Soup Noodle **26**
酸菜魚鬆麵 ....Sour Mustard and Fish Soup Noodle **27**
宋嫂麵 ....Madam Sung's Fish Soup Noodle **28**
揚州餃麵 ....Yang Chow Dumpling Soup Noodle **29**
五彩麵線 ....Five-Colored Soup Noodle String **30**
廈門麵線 ....Amoy's Speciality Soup Noodle String **31**
紅燒牛筋麵 ....Beef Tendon Stew Soup Noodle **32**
紅燒牛筋刀削麵 ....Beef Tendon Stew Soup Shaved Noodle **33**
沙嗲牛肉麵 ....Satay Beef Soup Noodle **34**
沙嗲牛肉刀削麵 ....Satay Beef Soup Shaved Noodle **35**
牛肉鍋燒麵 ....Beef Soup Udon in pot **36**
柱侯牛腩麵 ....Chee Ho Sauce and Beef Soup Noodle **37**
柱侯牛腩刀削麵 ....Chee Ho Sauce and Beef Soup Shaved Noodle **37**
蒜燒小排麵 ....Garlic Rib Soup Noodle **38**
醬味湯麵 ....Soy Bean Flavored Soup Noodle **40**
醬味刀削湯麵 ....Soy Bean Flavored Soup Shaved Noodle **40**
雪菜肉絲煨麵 ....Pork and Pickled Green Soup Braised Noodle **41**
酥肉湯麵 ....Fried Pork Fillet Soup Noodle **42**
嫩雞煨麵 ....Chicken Soup Braised Noodle **43**
片兒川麵 ....Hangzhou Style Pork Soup Noodle **44**
番茄刀削麵 ....Tomato Soup Shaved Noodle **45**
番茄麵片湯 ....Tomato Soup Noodle Pieces **45**
番茄湯麵 ....Tomato Soup Noodle **45**
鳳梨苦瓜雞麵 ....Tropical Chicken Soup Noodle String **46**
原盅蔘雞麵 ....Steamed Ginseng Chicken Soup Noodle **46**

炒麵 • *Fried Noodle*

斑球兩面黃 ....Fish Fillet on Noodle Pancake **47**
鐵板蝦仁麵 ....Shrimp Noodle on Sizzling Platter **48**
干燒蝦仁伊麵 ....Shrimp E-Fu Noodle **50**
番茄蝦仁麵 ....Tomato and Shrimp Noodle **51**
鮮魷炸麵 ....Squid on Deep Fried Noodle **52**
鮮魷伊麵 ....Squid on E-Fu Noodle **52**
豆豉蛤蜊麵 ....Clam Noodle in Black Bean Sauce **53**
豆豉蛤蜊刀削麵 ....Clam Shaved Noodle in Black Bean Sauce **53**
鮮貝炒麵 ....Fresh Scallop Noodle **54**
鮮貝刀切麵 ....Scallop Handmade Noodle **55**
雙鮮炒麵 ....Pork and Shrimp Fried Noodle **56**
什錦伊麵 ....Mix-Fried E-Fu Noodle **57**
沙茶牛柳伊麵 ....Sha-Cha Beef E-Fu Noodle **58**
沙茶牛柳炸麵 ....Sha-Cha Beef on Deep Fried Noodle **58**
番茄牛肉炒麵 ....Tomato and Beef Fried Noodle **59**
番茄牛肉刀削炒麵 ....Tomato and Beef Fried Shaved Noodle **59**
木須肉炒麵 ....Mu-Shu Pork Noodle **60**
木須肉刀切麵 ....Mu-Shu Pork Handmade Noodle **60**
木須肉刀削麵 ....Mu-Shu Pork Shaved Noodle **60**
豬肉筍片炒麵 ....Pork and Bamboo Shoot Fried Noodle **61**
咖哩雞炒麵 ....Curry Chicken Fried Noodle **62**
雞火炒麵 ....Chicken and Ham Fried Noodle **63**
雞火伊麵 ....Chicken and Ham E-Fu Noodle **63**
羅漢齋炒麵 ....Vegetarian's Fried Noodle **64**
銀芽三絲麵 ....Three Shreds and Bean Sprout Noodle **65**
金華炒麵 ....Chin Hua Style Fried Noodle **66**
鮑魚銀芽麵 ....Abalone and Bean Sprout Fried Noodle **66**
福建炒麵 ....Fu Kien Style Fried Noodle **67**
廣州炒麵 ....Guang Zhou Style Fried Noodle **67**
揚州炒麵 ....Yang Zhou Style Fried Noodle **68**

燴羹麵 · *Potagé and Sauce Noodle*

蝦茸窩麵	Minced Shrimp Potagé Noodle	**69**
台式窩麵	Taiwanese Potagé Noodle	**70**
川味魚塊麵	Szechwan Fish Potagé Noodle	**72**
虱目魚羹麵	Milk Fish Potagé Noodle	**74**
蟹肉羹麵	Crab Meat Potagé Noodle	**75**
汆滷刀削麵	Toen-Lu Potagé Shaved Noodle	**76**
汆滷麵	Toen-Lu Potagé Noodle	**76**
汆滷貓耳朵	Toen-Lu Potagé Cat's Ears	**76**
酸辣雞丁麵	Spicy and Sour Chicken Potagé Noodle	**77**

乾拌麵 · *Mixed Noodle*

蝦仁菠菜麵	Shrimp Spinach Noodle	**78**
青豆鮪魚拌麵	Tuna Fish Noodle	**79**
白果辣醬拌麵	Spicy Ginkgo Nut Noodle	**80**
生菜肉醬麵	Lettuce and Pork Sauce Noodle	**81**
臘腸撈麵	Sausage Lou Mein	**82**
豉汁排骨麵	Pork Rib in Black Bean Sauce Noodle	**83**
豉汁排骨撈麵	Pork Rib in Black Bean Sauce Lou Mein	**83**
豉汁雞撈麵	Chicken in Black Bean Sauce Lou Mein	**84**
豉汁雞拌麵	Chicken in Black Bean Sauce Noodle	**84**
蠔油芥菜拌麵	Mustard Green and Oyster Sauce Noodle	**85**
蠔油芥藍撈麵	Gailan and Oyster Sauce Lou Mein	**85**
蠔油芥藍拌麵	Gailan and Oyster Sauce Noodle	**85**

涼麵 · *Cold Noodle*

海鮮涼麵	Seafood Cold Noodle	**86**
五彩涼麵	Five-Colored Cold Noodle	**87**
牛筋涼麵	Beef Tendon Noodle	**88**
四彩涼麵	Four-Colored Cold Noodle	**88**
翡翠涼麵	Green Jade Noodle	**89**
棒棒雞麵	Bon Bon Chicken Noodle	**89**
怪味雞涼麵	Mix-Flavored Chicken Noodle	**90**
四川涼麵	Szechwan Style Cold Noodle	**91**
什錦涼麵	Mixed Cold Noodle	**92**
紅燒涼麵	Pork Soy Sauce Noodle	**93**

重量換算表 • *Measurement Equivalents*

1磅 = 454公克 = 16盎士   1lb.= 454gm (454g.) = 16oz.

1盎士 = 28.4公克   1oz. = 28.4gm (28.4g.)

量器說明 • *Table of Measurements*

1杯 = 236c.c. = 1 cup (1C.)

1大匙 = 1湯匙 = 15c.c. = 1 Tablespoon (1T.)

1小匙 = 1茶匙 = 5c.c. = 1 Teaspoon (1t.)

麵體製作 · *Methods of Noodle Making*

雞蛋麵 · *Egg Noodle*

低筋麵粉 ------- ３００公克	300g.(10½oz.) -----low gluten flour	
高筋麵粉 ------- １００公克	100g.(3½oz.) ------ high gluten flour	
雞蛋 --------------------- 3個	3 --------------------eggs	
太白粉 ----------------- 適量	as needed - corn starch	

１{ 水 ----------- ４０公克
　 鹽 --------------- ½小匙

１{ •40g.(1²/₅oz.)water
　 •½t.salt

1

2

3

1 將麵粉過篩，置於容器內，入雞蛋和 **１** 料拌勻，拌勻後揉成均勻且光滑之麵糰，再蓋上擰乾的濕布巾，醒３０分鐘。

2 將麵糰分成兩份，桌上撒上太白粉，把麵糰分別擀成２０公分×３０公分之麵皮後，在麵皮上撒些太白粉，再用擀麵棍捲起反覆壓平，使麵皮擀成０·１５〜０·２公分厚的薄皮。

3 把擀好之麵皮折三摺，用刀切成０·２公分寬之細條，並撒上太白粉即可。

1 Sift flours and place in a large bowl. Add in eggs and **１** ; mix well with the flours and knead into a smooth dough. Cover with a damp towel and let it stand for 30 minutes.

2 Part the dough to two. Dust the table with corn starch and roll the dough into two 20 x 30 cm large sheets. Dust corn starch on the sheets, roll again and again with rolling pin until became 0.15 cm to 0.2 cm thin dough sheets.

3 Fold the sheets three times, and cut into 0.2 cm wide thin noodles. Dust on more corn starch to avoid sticking.

菠菜麵 • *Spinach Noodle*

低筋麵粉 ------- ２５０公克	250g.(8⁴/₅oz.) ------ low gluten flour
高筋麵粉 ------- １５０公克	150g.(5⅓oz.) ------ high gluten flour
菠菜 ------------ １００公克	100g.(3½oz.) -- spinach
鹽 ---------------------- ½小匙	½t. --------------------- salt
太白粉 ------------------ 適量	as needed - corn starch

1 2

3

1 菠菜去頭洗淨，切成２公分長段，加２００公克水用果汁機打成汁狀，再用濾網過濾去渣，汁液備用。

2 將麵粉及鹽過篩，置於容器內，入菠菜汁拌勻，再揉成均勻且光滑的麵糰，蓋上擰乾的濕布巾，醒１０～２０分鐘。

3 在桌上撲上少許的太白粉，把麵糰切成兩份後，分別擀成０‧２公分厚之大薄片，在麵皮上再撒少許的太白粉，折疊數層，切成０‧３公分寬之條狀即可。

■ 麵體之寬窄可依個人之喜好而定。

1 Wash spinach clean and trim off root; cut into 2 cm long sections. Add 200g.(7oz.) water and puree in juicer; sieve and discard dregs to be clear spinach juice.

2 Sift flour and salt, place into a large bowl; add in spinach juice and mix well, knead evenly into a smooth dough. Cover with damp cloth and let it stand for 10 - 20 minutes.

3 Dust a little corn starch on the working table, divide dough into two parts. Roll each into 0.2 cm thick large sheet. Dust again with a little corn starch. Fold into few layers and cut into 0.3 cm wide noodles.

■ The width of the noodle depends on personal.

麵片 • *Noodle Pieces*

中筋麵粉 ------- ４００公克　　400g.(14oz.) -------- all-purpose flour

1 麵粉過篩，置於容器內，加水２２５公克拌勻後揉成均勻且光滑之麵糰，再將麵糰搓成直徑約３公分之長條，入冷水泡２０分鐘，以增加麵糰之延展性。
2 清水入鍋煮開，取出麵糰以手拉成小薄片，入滾水中煮熟撈起即可。

1　2

1 Sift flour and place into a large bowl, pour in 225g.(8oz.) water. Mix well and then knead into a even and smooth dough. Then knead the dough into 3 cm diameter strip. Soak in cold water for 20 minutes to increase its elasticity.
2 Boil water in a large pot. Pull thin noodle pieces off the dough by hand. Cook in boiling water until done.

刀切麵 • *Handmade Noodle*

中筋麵粉 ------- ４００公克　　400g.(14oz.) -------- all-purpose flour

1⎰ 水 --------- ２００公克　　**1**⎰ •200g.(7oz.) water
　⎱ 鹽 -------------- ½小匙　　　⎱ •½t.salt

1 麵粉過篩，置於容器內，入**1**料拌勻，拌勻後揉成均勻且光滑之麵糰，蓋上擰乾的濕布巾，醒１０～２０分鐘，取出麵糰置於已撒上乾麵粉的桌面上，再撒些乾粉於麵糰，用擀麵棍壓成０．２公分厚之大薄片。
2 麵皮上再撒些乾麵粉，摺數摺後切成０．５公分寬之麵條即可。
■ 喜食麵體較Q者，揉麵時水可少放些，喜食麵體較軟者，揉麵時水可多放些。麵條之寬窄亦可依個人之喜好，切粗或切細。

1

2

1 Sift flour and place into a large bowl; pour in **1** and mix well. Then knead to a even and smooth dough. Cover with damp cloth and let it stand for 10 - 20 minutes. Dust some flour on a working table and the dough, roll the dough with rolling pin into a 0.2 cm thick large sheet.
2 Dust the sheet with some flour again and fold into few layers; then cut into 0.5 cm wide noodles.
■ If harder noodle desired, water may be reduced. Therefore, water may be increased if softer noodle favored. The width of the noodle also depends on personal taste; may be cut wider or narrower.

刀削麵 • *Shaved Noodle*

中筋麵粉 ------- ４０ ０公克

［１］[水 --------- １８０公克
　　 鹽 ---------------- ½小匙

400g.(14oz.) -------- all-purpose flour

［１］[•180g. (5⅓oz.) water
　　 •½t.salt

1

2

1 麵粉過篩，置於容器內，入 **［１］** 料拌勻，拌勻後揉成較硬且光滑之麵糰，再壓成１５～１８公分長之圓筒狀。

2 清水置鍋內煮沸，一手托著麵糰，一手持刀將麵削成長１２～１５公分、寬１公分、厚０·１～０·３公分的條狀，下鍋煮熟，撈起瀝乾水分即可。

1 Sift flour and place in a large bowl; pour in **［１］** and mix well. Knead until it turns into a hard and smooth dough; press it into a 15 - 18 cm long cylinder shape.

2 Bring water to boil in a large pot. Hold the dough with one hand, and the other hand shave the dough with a knife into 12 - 15 cm long, 1 cm wide, and 0.1 - 0.3 cm thick noodle. Boil in water until cooked. Lift out and drain.

貓耳朵 • *Cat's Ears*

中筋麵粉 ------- ４０ ０公克

［１］[熱水（８０℃）--------
　　　 ------------ ２０ ０公克
　　 鹽 ---------------- ½小匙

400g.(11¼oz.) ------ all-purpose flour

［１］[•200g.(6oz.) warm water(176°F or 80°C)
　　 •½t.salt

1

1 麵粉過篩，置於容器內，邊入**［１］**料邊用筷子拌勻，拌勻後揉成光滑的麵糰。

2 麵糰搓成直徑０·７公分寬之條狀，再切成０·５～１·０公克之小麵粒。

3 將麵粒置於工作檯上，用大姆指輕壓麵粒再拉捏，使麵粒成扁薄而微捲像貓耳朵的形狀即可。（為避免壓好之麵粒黏在一起，則撒些乾粉使之分開。）

2

3

1 Sift flour and place into a large bowl, pour in **［１］** and mix well with chopsticks. Then knead into a smooth dough.

2 Knead the dough into a 0.7 cm diameter wide strip; then cut into 0.5 - 1.0 g. small pieces.

3 Place dough pieces on a working table, press down on each piece with thumb and pull the sides out gently to resemble a cat's ear. (Dust with flour to avoid sticking.)

麵的煮法 • *Guide to Noodle Cooking Methods*

冷水煮麵 • *Boil Noodle*

1 10杯水入鍋，加½小匙鹽煮開，入麵條並用筷子攪散。
2 待麵煮開後，續入1杯冷水煮至大滾，待麵心熟透，撈起瀝乾，放入煮好之湯料內即為湯麵。
3 若作為炒麵，則把煮熟之麵條撈起用冷水沖涼後，再瀝乾入鍋內與炒料同炒即可。
4 若作為涼拌類，其做法有二：
4-❶ 將煮熟之麵條撈起淋上少許麻油，拌勻後把麵置於通風處吹涼，再拌上作料即可。
4-❷ 將煮熟之麵條撈起用冷開水沖涼後，淋上作料拌勻即可。
■ 若麵條較寬，則第二次加水要多些且煮開後再滾約2分鐘使麵心熟透，若用乾麵條時，則煮的時間需再延長3～6分鐘。(視麵條之寬窄而定)

1 Bring 10C. water and ½t. salt to boil; add in noodle and loosen with chop stick.
2 When noodle boiled, add in 1C. cold water; bring to boil again. When the center of noodle is cooked, remove and drain. Place noodle in soup to be soup noodle.
3 For fried noodle, rinse boiled noodle under cold water to cool; drain and fry with desired materials.
4 For cold and mixed noodle :
4-❶ Sprinkle boiled noodle with some sesame oil and mix well, place near a drafty spot to cool. Mix with desired sauce and serve.
4-❷ Rinse boiled noodle under cold water to cool, drain. Pour desired sauce over and mix well.
■ When boil wider noodle, add cold water twice; after the second boil, let it boil 2 minutes more to ensure the center of the noodle is thoroughly cooked. If dried noodle used, then the boiling time should even be 3 - 6 minutes longer (Depends on the width of the noodle.)

1

2

3

4

油麵煮法 • *Boil Yellow Noodle*

1 生油麵煮法：１０杯水加½小匙的鹽煮開，入生油麵並用筷子攪散，水開後，加１杯水，續煮至大滾，待麵心熟透，隨即撈起，用冷開水沖涼，瀝乾水分，拌上少許的沙拉油即可。

2 熟油麵煮法：若買回來即為煮熟的油麵，則食前再入開水中川燙一下或直接拿來炒 麵即可。（圖２中：① 為生油麵，② 為熟油麵。）

1

2 ① ①

1 Fresh yellow noodle: Bring 10C. water and ½t. salt to boil, add in noodle and loosen with chopsticks. After water boil again, add in 1C. cold water; bring to boil again. When the center of the noodle is thoroughly cooked, remove and drain. Rinse under cold water, drain, and mix with some salad oil.

2 Boiled yellow noodle: (Market sold yellow noodle ususally is already boiled.) Scald in boiling water before serving or directly use it for fried noodle. (illus. **2**, ❶ fresh yellow noodle. ❷ boiled yellow noodle.)

麵線煮法 • *Boil Noodle String*

1 淡味麵線煮法除不加鹽外其餘做法與冷水煮麵相同。

2 若為鹹味麵線，則鍋內入１２杯水，煮開後入麵線，其餘做法與冷水煮麵相同。 （圖２中：①為淡味黑麵線，② 為淡味白麵線， ③ 為鹹味白麵線。）

1

2

1 For unsalted noodle string, the method remains the same as boiled noodle except no salt added.

2 For salted noodle string, bring 12C. water to boil; add in noodle string. The rest remains the same as boiled noodle. (illus. **2**, ❶ unsalted black noodle string. ❷ unsalted white noodle string. ❸ salted white noodle string.)

炸麵 • *Deep Fried Noodle*

1 將陽春麵入沸水中並用筷子攪散煮片刻（約1分鐘），撈起瀝乾。

2 油3杯燒至160℃，入麵條炸，炸至一邊堅硬且呈金黃色時翻面炸，再炸至麵條兩面皆呈金黃色時，撈起瀝乾即可。

1 Drop noodle into boiling water and loosen with chopsticks (about 1 minute). Remove and drain.

2 Heat 3C. oil to 160℃ (320°F), fry noodle until hard and golden on one side. Turn and fry the other side. Remove and drain on paper towel.

1 2

伊麵 • *E-Fu Noodle*

1 使用雞蛋麵，其做法同炸麵。

1 Egg noodle is used. Deep fry egg noodle as above to make e-fu noodle.

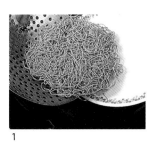

1

兩面黃 • *Noodle Pancake*

1 將麵條入沸水中並用筷子攪散煮片刻（約10秒），續入1杯冷水煮至大滾，撈起瀝乾，加少許沙拉油、醬油、麻油拌勻備用。

2 平底鍋燒熱入2大匙的沙拉油，把1項之麵條入鍋煎，並不時搖動鍋子，避免黏鍋，再逐次添加少許的沙拉油，用中火煎至麵條兩面呈金黃色且香脆即可。

■ 兩面黃可用陽春麵或雞蛋麵製作，但以雞蛋麵的效果較佳。

1 Drop noodle into boiling water and loosen with chopsticks (about 10 seconds), add in 1C. cold water and bring to boil again. Remove and drain. Mix in some salad oil, soy sauce, and sesame oil.

2 Heat a skillet, add 2T. oil; fry **1** noodle. Shake the skillet constantly to avoid sticking. Add in a little more oil during frying if needed. Fry over medinum heat until golden on both sides.

■Noodle pancake may be made from plain noodle or egg noodle, but egg noodle usually results the best.

1

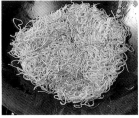

2

材料的前處理 • *Preparation of Special Food Materials*

花枝的處理 • *Squid*

1 花枝去皮、頸。
2 去除內臟，並用水洗淨。
3 花枝肉之內面，每隔0‧3公分縱橫切入⅓深度，使肉身作交叉片狀。
4 將片狀花枝切成4公分寬之條狀。
5 每一條花枝肉再切成4×5公分之片狀。

1 Discard the neck and peel off the skin.
2 Discard the inner gut and wash clean.
3 Score inner surface lengthwise and crosswise every 0.3 cm and ⅓ deep into the flesh.
4 Cut into 4 cm wide large strips.
5 Then cut each strip into 4 x 5 cm serving pieces.

1

2

3

4

5

海參的發法 • *Dried Sea Cucumber*

1 乾海參洗淨，泡水一天，隔天換水煮開，煮開後熄火浸泡，待水涼再換水煮開，熄火浸泡，如此一天3次，連續發兩天至軟。
2 由腹部剪開，取出內臟洗淨，加水煮開，再發一天即可。
3 若買發好之海參，則剪開肚子取出內臟洗淨即可。

1 Wash the dried sea cucumber clean, soak in water for one day. Place sea cucumber into new clean water and bring to boil; turn off the heat and soak until water cools. Change again to new clean water and bring to boil; turn off the heat and continue soaking until water cools. Repeat the process 3 times a day for 2 days until sea cucumber softened.
2 Snip open lengthwise and clean out the intestines. Cover with water and bring to boil. Remove from heat and let it stand for one more day. Then it is ready for cooking.
3 Already soaked sea cucumber can also be bought, then only need to snip open lengthwise and clean out the intestines.

1

2

3

蝦仁清洗方法 • *Shrimp*

1 蝦仁用牙籤由背面挑去腸泥（若帶殼，則先去殼）。
2 加太白粉、鹽，輕輕拌勻。
3 用清水洗淨，瀝乾。

1 Devine the shrimp with toothpick (must be shelled first).
2 Clean shrimp by rubbing gently with corn starch and salt.
3 Rinse under water and drian.

1   2

3

海蜇皮的處理 • *Jelly Fish*

1 海蜇皮先洗淨，切絲泡冷水，泡水時需不斷換水，以去鹹味。
2 海蜇皮入半滾水中川燙，隨即撈出，再浸泡冷水至柔軟即可使用。

1 Wash jelly fish clean, shred and soak in water. Change water often to rid of the salty taste.
2 Scald jelly fish in half-boiling water; lift out immediately. Soak in cold water again until softened.

1   2

牛筋的處理 • *Beef Tendon*

1 水一大鍋煮沸後，加少許的蔥、薑、酒、及牛筋煮約5小時至爛即可，過程中若有白色渣渣出現，則用杓子撈掉。
■ 若用壓力鍋煮則約需3小時。

1 Bring a large pot of water to boil, add a little green onion, ginger, cooking wine, and beef tendon in to simmer for 5 hours or until tender. Skim off the white foam during simmering.
■ If pressure cooker used, 3 hours will be sufficient.

1

薑泥和薑汁的製作 • *Ginger Paste and Ginger Juice*

1 薑洗淨，去皮。
2 用磨泥板磨成泥，即為薑泥，再過濾去渣即為薑汁。

1 Wash ginger clean and trim off skin.
2 Rub on a mash board to finely mashed ginger; It is ginger paste. Sieve and discard the sediments to be clear ginger juice.

1　2

蒜泥的製作 • *Garlic Paste*

1 蒜洗淨，去皮。
2 用磨泥板磨成泥即可。

1 Wash garlic clean, peel off skin.
2 Rub on a mash board to finely mashed garlic.

1　2

銀芽 • *Bean Sprout*

1 將綠豆芽之頭、尾去除，謂之銀芽。

1 Discard the bean tip and root.

1

筍的處理 • *Bamboo Shoot*

1 新鮮筍去殼，入水中煮至熟，再取出漂涼即可，若是罐頭筍，有些因製罐關係，會帶有些微酸味，可以先入鍋川燙以去酸味。

1 Peel off the hard shell; boil until cooked, drain and cool. If canned bamboo used, it will be slightly sour; parboil in boiling water to rid of sour taste before cooking.

1

蔥段的切法 • *Green Onion Sections*

1 蔥洗淨。
2 去頭、尾部分。
3 切成3公分長段。

1 Wash green onion clean.
2 Trim off the tops and roots.
3 Cut into 3 cm long sections.

1

2

3

洋菇的處理 • *Mushroom*

1 若新鮮洋菇則需先入開水中煮熟,再取出漂涼,即為熟洋菇。
2 若罐頭洋菇,則開罐後瀝乾水分,再用沸水漂過即可使用。

1 Fresh mushroom needs to be boiled first, then rinse under cold water.
2 If canned mushroom used, drain; and then rinse with boiling water.

1

2

番茄的處理 • *Tomato*

1 番茄洗淨,表面劃米字,入沸水中煮至皮開,撈起漂涼,瀝乾再去皮。
2 將番茄橫切,把籽去掉即可。

1 Wash tomato clean; score a cross on the surface. Place in boiling water until skin opens. Lift out and cool. Peel.
2 Cut tomato widthwise and discard the seeds.

1

2

烹調的方法・*Guide to Cooking Terms*

上湯的製作・*Consommé*

1 雞、豬、中式火腿的肉切成 3～4 公分之小塊，入沸水中川燙後取出洗淨。

2 以另一鍋水燒開再入洗淨的肉，並加少許胡椒粒、陳皮，慢火熬出來的湯，謂之上湯。

1 Cut chicken, pork, and Chinese ham into 3 - 4 cm cubes; parboil in boiling water. Lift out and rinse clean.

2 Bring a pot of water to boil, add in parboiled meats with a pinch of pepper corn and dried orange peel. Simmer over low heat until the consommé is tasty.

1

2

高湯的製作・*Stock*

1 以豬、牛、雞的肉或骨入沸水中川燙。

2 再將肉或骨頭取出洗淨。

3 以另一鍋水燒開，再入洗淨的肉或骨頭，並加少許蔥、薑、酒，慢火熬出來的湯，謂之高湯。

■ 本書使用之高湯為依此法所製之高湯，若使用市售之高湯製作麵食，則需再降低鹽及味精的用量。

1 Parboil pork, beef, chicken or bones.

2 Lift out and rinse clean.

3 Bring new clean water to boil, add in meat or bones together with a little green onion, ginger, and cooking wine. Simmer over low heat until the stock is tasty.

■ If can broth is used, seasonings may be reduced.

1

2   3

煮出汁的製作 • *Seaweed Stock*

1 乾海帶（2公克）用布擦乾淨，剪成1公分寬之條狀。
2 鍋內入水兩杯及海帶，煮至快沸騰時取出海帶，續入柴魚片
　（10公克）並立即熄火，待柴魚片沈澱後過濾，此即為煮
　出汁。

1 Wipe dried seaweed (2g.) clean with a cloth; snip into 1 cm wide strips.
2 Add 2C. water and seaweed in a pot, cook until nearly to boiling point. Lift out seaweed, add in dried fish flakes (10g. or ⅓ oz.) and turn off heat immediately. When fish flakes sink to the bottom of the stock, sieve to be clear seaweed stock.

1　2

川燙 • *Parboil*

1 鍋水以大火煮沸。
2 放入材料再煮沸，隨即撈起。
3 漂冷水。

1 Bring water to boil over high heat.
2 Add in material and bring to boil once again. Quickly lift out.
3 Rinse under cold water.

1　2

3

過油 • *Hot Oil Soaking*

1 將食物泡入熱油內（五分熱120℃），食物剛熟即刻撈
　出，時間不可過長，謂之過油。

1 Soak material into semi-hot oil (248°F/120°C), lift out as soon as material is cooked. It should be done in a minimum time required.

1

各種麵體的說明與換算

1 自製生麵重：是指家庭手工所製成麵條之生重。
2 市售生乾麵：是市場所賣經過烘乾加工，麵體直而堅硬且包裝完整之生麵。
3 市售生濕麵：是市場所賣未經烘乾加工，麵體較軟且形狀無法固定之生麵。
4 市售熟麵：是指市場所賣經煮熟後再冷卻之熟麵條，如一般之油麵及烏龍麵等。
5 熟重：意指經本文所介紹麵的煮法煮熟之麵體重。
6 本食譜所指陽春麵即為市售之生白麵條。
7 日式素麵：即為市售之日本麵，其麵體色白且較陽春麵為細。
8 廈門麵線：與白麵線相似，只是麵體比較細。
9 以下所指麵體重皆以一人份為準。

麵體名稱	自製生麵重	市售生乾麵重	市售生溼麵重	市售熟麵重	熟重
1. 刀削麵	135公克				220公克
2. 刀切麵	150公克				220公克
3. 麵片	160公克				220公克
4. 雞蛋麵	150公克	90公克	120公克		220公克
5. 伊麵			100公克		90公克
6. 炸麵			100公克		90公克
7. 兩面黃			120公克		170公克
8. 貓耳朵	135公克				200公克
9. 菠菜麵	150公克	90公克			220公克
10. 陽春麵		90公克	120公克		220公克
11. 烏龍麵				220公克	
12. 油麵		90公克		220公克	200公克
13. 意麵			120公克		220公克
14. 黑麵線			70公克		190公克
15. 白麵線		75公克	90公克		220公克
16. 廈門麵線		75公克	90公克		220公克
17. 蕎麥麵		80公克	110公克		200公克
18. 拉麵		90公克	120公克		220公克
19. 日式素麵		80公克			220公克

General Information on Noodle Weight Equivalent Chart:

1 Weight of uncooked homemade fresh noodles: It means the weight of uncooked freshly homemade and usually handmade noodles.

2 Weight of uncooked dehydrated noodles: Uncooked dehydrated noodles are processed through dehydration. Usually straight and hard, they are sold in the manufacturer's package at markets. This means the weight of raw noodles before cooking.

3 Weight of uncooked freshly made noodles: Applies to market purchased fresh noodles which have not been processed, are usually wet and soft, and sometimes have no certain forms or shapes. This means the weight of the noodles before cooking.

4 Weight of ready-made noodles: Applies to market purchased noodles which are ready cooked and cooled, such as yellow noodles or udon. This means the weight of purchased amount.

5 Weight after cooking: Means the weight of the noodles after preparation according to cooking instructions in this book.

6 Plain noodles used in this cook book refers to market purchased white, uncooked,fresh,round noodles of medium thickness.

7 Japanese So Mein: Market purchased Japanese noodles, which are whiter and thinner than plain noodles.

8 Amoy noodle string: Similar to white noodle string, but even thinner.

9 All the weights indicated below are for one serving.

Name	Weight of un-cooked home-made noodles	Weight of un-cooked dehy-drated noodles	Weight of un-cooked freshly made noodles	Weight of ready-made noodles	Weight after cooking
1.Shaved noodles	135g (4 ³/₄ oz.)				220g (7 ³/₄ oz.)
2.Handmade noodles	150g (5 ¹/₃ oz.)				220g (7 ³/₄ oz.)
3.Noodle pieces	160g (5 ³/₅ oz.)				220g (7 ³/₄ oz.)
4.Egg noodles	150g (5 ¹/₃ oz.)	90g (3 ¹/₅ oz.)	120g (4 ¹/₄ oz.)		220g (7 ³/₄ oz.)
5.E-fu noodles			100g (3 ¹/₂ oz.)		90g (3 ¹/₅ oz.)
6.Deep fried noodles			100g (3 ¹/₂ oz.)		90g (3 ¹/₅ oz.)
7.Noodle pancake			120g (4 ¹/₄ oz.)		170g (6 oz.)
8.Cat's ears	135g (4 ³/₄ oz.)				220g (7 oz.)
9.Spinach noodles	150g (5 ¹/₃ oz.)	90g (3 ¹/₅ oz.)			220g (7 ³/₄ oz.)
10.Plain noodles		90g (3 ¹/₅ oz.)	120g (4 ¹/₄ oz.)		220g (7 ³/₄ oz.)
11.Udon				220g (7 ³/₄ oz.)	
12.Yellow noodles		90g (3 ¹/₅ oz.)		220g (7 ³/₄ oz.)	200g (7 oz.)
13.Yi-mein			120g (4 ¹/₄ oz.)		220g (7 ³/₄ oz.)
14.Black noodle string			70g (2 ¹/₂ oz.)		190g (6 ²/₃ oz.)
15.White noodle string		75g (2 ²/₃ oz.)	90g (3 ¹/₅ oz.)		220g (7 ³/₄ oz.)
16.Amoy noodle string		75g (2 ²/₃ oz.)	90g (3 ¹/₅ oz.)		220g (7 ³/₄ oz.)
17.Buckwheat noodles		80g (2 ⁴/₅ oz.)	110g (4 oz.)		200g (7 oz.)
18.Hand pulled noodles		90g (3 ³/₅ oz.)	120g (4 ¹/₄ oz.)		220g (7 ³/₄ oz.)
19.Japanese So Mein		80g (2 ⁴/₅ oz.)			220g (7 ³/₄ oz.

斑球伊麵

.Fish Fillet Soup E-Fu Noodle

四人份　**serve　4**

斑球伊麵 · *Fish Fillet Soup E-Fu Noodle*

伊麵	３６０公克
白色魚肉淨重	２００公克
小白菜	１２０公克
綠蘆筍	８０公克
熟筍、胡蘿蔔	各６０公克
高湯	８杯
蔥段	１２段
蔥末	５大匙
玉米粉	２大匙
薑片	２片

360g.(12²/₃oz.)	e-fu noodle
200g.(7oz.)	white meat fish fillet (net weight)
120g.(4¼oz.)	baby cabbage
80g.(2⁴/₅oz.)	green asparagus
60g.(2¹/₉oz.)each	canned bamboo shoot, carrot
8C.	stock
12 sections	green onion
5T.	minced green onion
2T.	corn starch
2 slices	ginger

1
- 太白粉、酒、蛋白 --- 各１小匙
- 鹽 --- ¼小匙
- 味精、胡椒粉 --- 各⅛小匙

3
- 水 --- ２大匙
- 太白粉 --- １大匙

2
- 水 --- ３大匙
- 糖 --- ½小匙
- 鹽、味精 --- 各¼小匙
- 胡椒粉 --- ⅛小匙

4
- 鹽 --- １¼小匙
- 味精、酒、麻油 各½小匙
- 胡椒粉 --- ⅛小匙

1
- •1t.each corn starch, cooking wine, egg white
- •¼t.salt
- •⅛t.pepper

2
- •3T.water
- •½t.sugar
- •¼t.salt
- •⅛t.pepper

3
- •2T.water
- •1T.corn starch

4
- •1¼t.salt
- •½t.each cooking wine, sesame oil
- •⅛t.pepper

1 將筍、胡蘿蔔切３×４公分薄片，蘆筍切２公分段，入鍋川燙，小白菜洗淨切段備用。

2 魚肉切４×６公分薄片，以 **1** 料醃３０分鐘後灑上玉米粉，捲成圓筒狀，鍋熱入油３杯燒至七分熱（１６０℃），入魚捲炸至金黃色撈起。

3 鍋內留油１大匙，入蔥段、薑片爆香，續入筍、胡蘿蔔、蘆筍拌炒，再加入魚捲及 **2** 料拌炒均勻後，以 **3** 料芶芡即為麵的配菜。

4 高湯煮開，入 **4** 料調味後，再入小白菜煮開即為麵湯。

5 伊麵置於碗中，上置配菜及蔥末，再淋上麵湯即可。

1 Cut bamboo and carrot into 3 x 4 cm thin slices, asparagus into 2 cm sections; scald in boiling water. Wash cabbage and cut into serving sections.

2 Cut fish fillet into 4 x 6 cm thin slices, marinate in **1** for 30 minutes; dust on corn starch and roll into cylinders. Heat the wok, add 3C. oil and heat to 160℃ (320°F). Drop in fish rolls and fry until golden.

3 Keep 1T. oil in the wok, stir fry green onion sections and ginger slices until fragrant. Add in bamboo, carrot, and asparagus to fry evenly. Mix in fish rolls and **2**, stir fry well. Thicken with **3** to be the noodle topping.

4 Bring stock to boil, season with **4**. Add in cabbage and bring to boil again to be the noodle soup.

5 Place e-fu noodle in individual bowls, arrange noodle topping on top and sprinkle on minced green onion. Pour noodle soup over and serve.

銀魚湯麵

.Silver Fish Soup Noodle

四人份   serve   4

銀魚湯麵 • *Silver Fish Soup Noodle*

熟陽春麵 ----------- 880公克
大尾銀魚 ----------- 150公克
韭菜花 ------------- 120公克
紅蔥頭 ------------- 20公克
紅辣椒 ------------- 15公克
高湯 ---------------- 8杯
蔥末 ---------------- 5大匙
太白粉 -------------- 2大匙

1
低筋麵粉 ------------- ²/₃杯
水 -------------------- ½杯
太白粉 -------------- 4大匙
泡打粉 -------------- ½小匙
鹽 ------------------- ¼小匙
蛋 ------------------- 1個

2
酒 ------------------- 1小匙
鹽、胡椒粉、味精 --------
-------------------- 各⅛小匙

3
酒 ------------------ 2小匙
鹽 ------------------ ½小匙
味精 ---------------- ¼小匙
胡椒粉 -------------- ⅛小匙

1 韭菜花洗淨切4公分長段，紅辣椒洗淨切小圓圈狀，紅蔥頭洗淨切末。
2 銀魚洗淨加 **2** 料醃約30分鐘，再灑上太白粉，**1** 料調勻成麵糊備用。
3 鍋熱入油3杯燒至六分熱（140℃），銀魚裹上麵糊入鍋中炸至金黃色撈起。
4 鍋中留油2大匙，爆香紅蔥頭末，續入韭菜花、紅辣椒拌炒均勻盛起。
5 麵條置於碗中，高湯煮開入 **3** 料及 **4** 項之材料略煮一下，淋於麵上，上置炸好的銀魚並灑上蔥末即可。

880g.(2lb.) ----------------------------boiled plain noodle
150g.(5⅓oz.) ----------------------------large silver fish
120g.(4¼oz.) ----------------------chive with flowering tip
20g.(²/₃oz.) ----------------------------------red shallot
15g.(½oz.) -----------------------------------red pepper
8C. ---stock
5T. -----------------------------------minced green onion
2T. --corn starch

1
• ²/₃C.low gluten flour
• ½C.water
• 4T.corn starch
• ½t.baking powder
• ¼t.salt
• 1 egg

2
• 1t.cooking wine
• ⅛t.each salt, pepper

3
• 2t.cooking wine
• ½t.salt
• ⅛t.pepper

1 Wash chive clean and cut into 4 cm long sections. Wash red pepper clean and cut into small circles. Wash shallot and mince.
2 Wash silver fish clean and marinate in **2** for 30 minutes, then dust on corn starch. Mix all ingredients in **1** well into a flour paste.
3 Heat the wok, add 3C. oil and heat to 140°C (284°F). Coat silver fish with flour paste. Fry in oil until golden. Drain.
4 Keep 2T. oil in the wok, stir fry shallot until fragrant; add in chive and red pepper. Mix well and remove.
5 Place noodle in individual bowls. Bring stock to boil, season with **3**; add in **4** and simmer for a while. Pour over noodle. Arrange fried fish on the noodle, sprinkle on minced green onion and serve.

黃魚煨麵・*Yellow Fish Braised Soup Noodle*

熟陽春麵	880公克	薑絲	20公克
黃魚	650公克	上湯	9杯
雪裡紅	320公克	蔥段	20段

❶
- 酒 ------------------- 2小匙
- 鹽、麻油 -------- 各1小匙
- 味精 ------------------ ²/₃小匙
- 胡椒粉 -------------- ¼小匙

1 黃魚去鱗、鰓、內臟後洗淨，從中剖成兩半並去大骨，以鐵湯匙刮下魚肉並去小骨頭，雪裡紅洗淨切末備用。

2 鍋熱入油3大匙燒熱，入蔥段、薑絲爆香後再入黃魚、雪菜炒熟後取出備用。

3 砂鍋內加入上湯煮開，再入麵條煮3分鐘後，續入 **❶** 料及雪菜黃魚，再燜煮5分鐘即可。

880g.(2lb.) --- boiled plain noodle
650g.(1²/₅lb.) - yellow fish
320g.(14oz.) ------ pickled mustard green

20g.(²/₃oz.) ------ shredded ginger
9C. ------------ consommé
20 sections -- green onion

❶
- •2t.cooking wine
- •1t.each salt, sesame oil
- •¼t.pepper

1 Scrape off scales on yellow fish, discard gill and internal organs; rinse clean. Cut fish lengthwise to halves, remove the center bone. With a metal spoon scrape off fish meat and remove smaller bones. Wash pickled mustard green clean and chop fine.

2 Heat the wok, add 3T. oil and heat to hot; stir fry green onion and shredded ginger until fragrant. Add in fish meat and pickled mustard green, stir fry until cooked. Remove.

3 Bring consommé to boil in a ceramic pot, add in noodle and boil for 3 minutes. Season with **❶** and arrange fish meat with pickled mustard green on top, simmer for 5 minutes. Serve directly form the pot.

酸菜魚鬆麵 • *Sour Mustard and Fish Soup Noodle*

熟陽春麵 ----------- 880公克	高湯 ------------------------- 8杯	
白色魚肉 ----------- 280公克	蔥段 ------------------------ 20段	
酸菜（或雪裡紅）240公克		

1
- 蛋白 -------------------- 1個
- 太白粉 ----------------- 2小匙
- 酒 ------------------------ 1小匙
- 鹽 ------------------------ 1/4小匙
- 胡椒粉、味精 ---各1/8小匙

2
- 酒、雞油 -------- 各2小匙
- 鹽 -------------------- 1小匙
- 味精 ----------------- 1/4小匙
- 胡椒粉 -------------- 1/8小匙

3
- 水 -------------------- 2大匙
- 太白粉 ------------- 1大匙

1 魚肉切成1公分立方丁塊，入**1**料醃30分鐘，酸菜洗淨切末。
2 鍋熱入油3杯燒至五分熱（120℃），入魚肉炸熟撈起瀝油。
3 鍋中留油2大匙，入蔥段、酸菜略炒，再入魚肉拌炒盛起，即為酸菜魚鬆。
4 麵條置於碗中，高湯加**2**料煮開，並以**3**料芶芡後淋於麵上，再加入酸菜魚鬆即可。

880g.(2lb.) ---boiled plain noodle
280g.(9 4/5 oz.) -------- white meat fish fillet
240g.(8 2/5 oz.) --------- sour mustard or pickled mustard green
8C. --------------------- stock
20 sections -- green onion

1
- 1 egg white
- 2t.corn starch
- 1t.cooking wine
- 1/4t.salt
- 1/8t.pepper

2
- 2t.each cooking wine, chicken fat
- 1t.salt
- 1/8t.pepper

3
- 2T.water
- 1T.corn starch

1 Dice fish fillet into 1 cm square cubes, marinate in **1** for 30 minutes. Wash sour mustard clean and mince.
2 Heat the wok, add 3C. oil and heat to 120℃ (248°F). Fry fish until cooked, remove and drain.
3 Keep 2T. oil in the wok, stir fry green onion sections and sour mustard for a while. Add in fish to fry and mix well.
4 Place noodle in individual bowls. Season stock with **2** and bring to boil, thicken with **3**. Pour over noodle, arrange fish fiber and serve.

宋嫂麵 · *Madam Sung's Fish Soup Noodle*

熟陽春麵 ----------- ８８０公克	**1**⎡ 蛋白 ------------------ ½個
	  ⎢ 太白粉 ------------- １大匙
	  ⎣ 鹽、胡椒粉、酒 各⅛小匙	

鮮鯉魚１尾 ------ 約４５０公克		
芥藍菜 ------------- １４０公克		

蝦仁 ----------------- ４０公克	**2**⎡ 豆瓣醬 ------------- １大匙
	  ⎢ 鹽、烏醋 ------ 各１½小匙
	  ⎢ 味精 ----------------- ¼小匙
	  ⎣ 胡椒粉 -------------- ⅛小匙	

香菇 ------------------- ８公克		
高湯 ------------------- １２杯		
榨菜末 ---------------- ½杯		
蔥末 ------------------- ５大匙	**3**⎡ 水 ------------------- ２大匙 ⎣ 太白粉 ------------ １大匙	
薑末 ------------------- ½大匙		

1 鯉魚從背脊切開，去除內臟，魚皮、魚骨留用，魚肉切２公分立方小丁，以 **1** 料醃拌約２０分鐘，蝦仁去腸泥洗淨切１公分立方小丁。

2 鍋熱入油２杯燒至七分熱（１６０℃），入魚塊、蝦仁過油撈起，芥藍菜洗淨切段，香菇泡軟去蒂切小丁，兩者均以川燙備用。

3 鍋熱入油３大匙燒熱，入 **2** 料炒香後續入魚皮、骨、薑末拌炒，隨即入高湯煮開後改小火煮約３０分鐘，撈去渣質，再放入蝦仁、芥藍菜、香菇煮約１５分鐘，並以 **3** 料芶芡即為麵湯。

4 麵條置於碗中，灑上榨菜末、蔥末及魚肉並淋上麵湯即可。

880g.(2lb.) ---boiled plain noodle		**1**⎡ •½ egg white
		  ⎢ •1T.corn starch
		  ⎢ •⅛t.each salt, pepper,
		  ⎣ cooking wine

450g.(1lb.) one fresh carp		
140g.(5oz.) ---------- gailan		
40g.(1²/₅oz.) -------- shelled shrimp		

8g.(¼oz.) ------ dried black mushroom		**2**⎡ •1T.soy bean paste
		  ⎢ •1½t.each salt,
		  ⎢ brown vinegar
		  ⎣ •⅛t.pepper

12C. ------------------- stock		
½C. -------- minced pickled mustard head		
5T. --minced green onion		**3**⎡ •2T.water ⎣ •1T.corn starch
½T. --------- minced ginger		

1 Snip carp open on the back spine, discard all internal organs; remove skin and center bone for later use. Dice fish meat into 2 cm cubes, marinate in **1** for 20 minutes. Devein shrimp, rinse clean, and cut into 1 cm cubes.

2 Heat the wok, add 3C. oil and heat to 160°C (320°F). Soak fish and shrimp in hot oil, lift out immediately. Wash gailan clean and cut into serving sections. Soften black mushroom in warm water, discard stem, and dice. Scald both in boiling water.

3 Heat the wok, add 3T. oil and heat to hot. Stir fry **2** until fragrant, add in fish skin, fish bone, and minced ginger to fry. Pour in stock and bring to boil; turn the heat to low and simmer for 30 minutes. Strain the soup clear, add in shrimp, gailan, and mushroom to simmer for 15 minutes. Thicken with **3** to be the fish soup.

4 Place noodle in individual bowls, sprinkle on minced pickled mustard head, minced greeen onion, and fish. Pour over fish soup and serve.

揚州餃麵 · *Yang Chow Dumpling Soup Noodle*

熟陽春麵 ----------- 880公克	
絞肉 --------------- 170公克	
小白菜 ------------- 160公克	
蝦仁 ----------------- 50公克	
榨菜、芹菜 -------- 各20公克	
水餃皮 --------------- 16張	
高湯 ------------------- 9杯	
草蝦 ------------------- 8隻	
蔥末 ----------------- 1¼大匙	

1
- 蔥末 ------------- 1¼大匙
- 薑末 -------------- ½大匙

2
- 麻油 ------------- 1大匙
- 鹽 --------------- ½小匙
- 味精 ------------- ¼小匙
- 胡椒粉 ----------- ⅛小匙

3
- 麻油 ------------- 2小匙
- 鹽 -------------- 1½小匙
- 味精 ------------- ¼小匙
- 胡椒粉 ----------- ⅛小匙

880g.(2lb.) --- boiled plain noodle
170g.(6oz.) - minced pork
160g.(5⅗oz.) --------- baby cabbage
50g.(1¾oz.) -------- shelled shrimp
20g.(⅔oz.)each --- pickled mustard head, celery
16 pieces -- dumpling skin
9C. --------------------- stock
8 --------- large fresh water shrimp
1¼T. minced green onion

1
- •1¼T.minced green onion
- •½T.minced ginger

2
- •1T.sesame oil
- •½t.salt
- •⅛t.pepper

3
- •2t.sesame oil
- •1½t.salt
- •⅛t.pepper

1 蝦仁去腸泥洗淨與榨菜、芹菜切末後與絞肉、**1** 料及 **2** 料拌勻為餃子餡,再以水餃皮包成餃子。
2 草蝦去鬚腳洗淨,小白菜洗淨切段。
3 高湯煮開,入餃子煮熟後續入草蝦煮熟,加 **3** 料調味,再加入小白菜煮開即為麵湯。
4 麵條置於碗中,淋上麵湯並灑上蔥末即可。

1 Devein shrimp and rinse clean; chop fine with pickled mustard head and celery. Mix with minced pork, **1**, and **2** to be the dumpling filling. Wrap in dumpling skin.
2 Snip off feelers and legs of fresh water shrimp, rinse clean. Wash baby cabbage clean and cut into serving sections.
3 Bring stock to boil, drop dumpling in until cooked. Add in fresh water shrimp to boil until cooked. Season with **3**, add in baby cabbage, and bring to boil again to be noodle soup.
4 Place noodle in individual bowls, pour noodle soup over, and sprinkle on minced green onion. Serve.

五彩麵線 · *Five-Colored Soup Noodle String*

熟白麵線 ------------ ８８０公克	胡蘿蔔絲、蔥綠絲 各３０公克
草蝦 ------------------ ３２０公克	香菇、薑絲 ----------- 各８公克
洋火腿絲 ------------ １００公克	上湯 ----------------------- ８杯
熟洋菇、菜心 ------ 各６０公克	蔥末 ----------------------- １大匙
酸菜絲 ----------------- ５０公克	

1
- 蛋白 ------------------- ½個
- 玉米粉 ---------------- １小匙
- 鹽、味精 -------- 各¼小匙
- 胡椒粉 --------------- ⅛小匙

2
- 醬油 ----------------- １大匙
- 鹽、麻油 -------- 各１小匙
- 酒、味精 -------- 各½小匙
- 胡椒粉 --------------- ⅛小匙

1 草蝦去頭入上湯中熬煮片刻後，撈去蝦頭。
2 蝦去殼、去腸泥洗淨，由背部劃開，加 **1** 料醃３０分鐘備用。
3 菜心去皮切１×４公分條狀，香菇泡軟去蒂切絲。
4 鍋熱入油３大匙燒熱，入蔥、薑及香菇炒香，再入胡蘿蔔、洋菇、菜心、火腿絲及酸菜絲略炒並加上湯及 **2** 料煮開，再加入蝦仁煮熟即為麵湯。
5 麵線置於碗中，上置蔥綠絲再淋上麵湯即可。

880g.(2lb.) --boiled white noodle string
320g.(11¼oz.) ------- large fresh water shrimp
100g.(3½oz.) ---shredded virginia ham
60g.(2⅑oz.)each --canned mushroom,mustard stick
50g.(1¾oz.) -----shredded sour mustard

30g.(1oz.)each -shredded carrot,shredded green onion
8g.(¼oz.)each -------- dried black mushroom, shredded ginger
8C. ------------consommé
1T. --minced green onion

1
- ½ egg white
- 1t.corn starch
- ¼t.salt
- ⅛t.pepper

2
- 1T.soy sauce
- 1t.each salt, sesame oil
- ½t.cooking wine
- ⅛t.pepper

1 Snip off the head of shrimp, boil the shrimp heads in consommé for a while. Remove the shrimp heads.
2 Shell shrimp, devein, and rinse clean. Cut the back open and marinate in **1** for 30 minutes.
3 Peel skin off mustard stick, cut into 1 x 4 cm long strips. Soften dried black mushroom in warm water, discard stem, and shred.
4 Heat the wok, add 3T. oil and heat to hot; stir fry minced green onion, ginger, and black mushroom until fragrant. Add in carrot, mushroom, mustard stick, ham, and sour mustard to stir fry until evenly mixed. Pour in consommé and **2**, bring to boil. Stir in shrimp, boil until cooked. This is the noodle soup.
5 Place noodle string in individual bowls, arrange shredded green onion on top. Pour noodle soup over and serve.

廈門麵線 • *Amoy's Speciality Soup Noodle String*

熟廈門麵線 -------- 880公克	香菇 ----------------------- 8公克	880g.(2lb.) --boiled Amoy noodle string	15g.(½oz.) -----dried baby shrimp
榨菜、小白菜 --- 各240公克	高湯 ----------------------- 8杯	240g.(8²/₅oz.)each pickled mustard head,baby cabbage	8g.(¼oz.) ------dried black mushroom
里肌肉 ------------- 200公克	蔥段 ----------------------- 15段		8C. --------------------stock
蝦米 --------------------- 15公克	蔥末 ----------------------- 5大匙	200g.(7oz.) -----pork fillet	15 sections --green onion
			5T. --minced green onion

1
┌ 太白粉 ------------- 1大匙
│ 麻油 --------------- 1小匙
│ 醬油、酒 --------- 各½小匙
└ 鹽、味精 --------- 各¼小匙

2
┌ 鹽 ----------------- 1¼小匙
│ 味精、麻油 ------ 各½小匙
└ 胡椒粉 -------------- ⅛小匙

1
- •1T.corn starch
- •1t.sesame oil
- •½t.each soy sauce, cooking wine
- •¼t.salt

2
- •1¼t.salt
- •½t.sesame oil
- •⅛t.pepper

1 里肌肉切絲，以 **1** 料醃約30分鐘，榨菜洗淨切絲，香菇泡軟去蒂切絲，蝦米洗淨泡軟，小白菜洗淨切段。

2 鍋熱入油4大匙燒熱，入蔥段、蝦米爆香，再入香菇略炒後，續入肉絲炒熟，再入高湯及 **2** 料煮開，最後入小白菜煮開即為麵湯。

3 麵線置於碗中，灑上蔥末及榨菜絲，再淋上麵湯即可。

1 Shred pork fillet and marinate in **1** for 30 minutes. Wash pickled mustard head and shred. Soften black mushroom in warm water, discard stem, and shred. Wash dried shrimp clean, and soften in warm water. Wash cabbage clean and cut into serving sections.

2 Heat the wok, add 4T. oil and heat to hot. Stir fry green onion sections and dried shrimp until fragrant. Add in black mushroom to fry for a while, then add in pork to fry until cooked. Pour in stock and **2**, bring to boil. Add in cabbage and bring to boil again. This is the noodle soup.

3 Place noodle string in individual bowls, sprinkle on minced green onion and shredded pickled mustard head. Pour noodle soup over and serve.

紅燒牛筋麵

•*Beef Tendon Stew Soup Noodle*

四人份　**serve　4**

紅燒牛筋麵 · *Beef Tendon Stew Soup Noodle*

熟陽春麵 ----------- ８８０公克
熟牛筋 ------------ ４００公克
箭竹筍 ------------ ２００公克
白蒟蒻 ------------ １８０公克
小白菜 ------------ １６０公克
胡蘿蔔 ------------- ６０公克
高湯 ------------- ８½杯
紅蔥頭末 ----------- １½大匙
蒜末 ---------------- １大匙

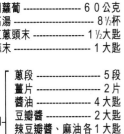

蔥段 ----------------- ５段
薑片 ----------------- ２片
醬油 ----------------- ４大匙
豆瓣醬 -------------- ２大匙
辣豆瓣醬、麻油各１大匙
紅糟、糖 -------- 各２小匙
味精 ----------------- ½小匙
胡椒粉 ------------- ¼小匙

1 熟牛筋切５×２公分長條狀，蒟蒻切２×５公分片狀，並在兩面切花，小白菜洗淨切５公分長段。

2 胡蘿蔔洗淨切２×４公分片狀，箭竹筍切４公分長段，兩者一起川燙備用。

3 鍋熱入油３大匙燒熱，入紅蔥頭末、蒜末爆香，續入牛筋、箭竹筍、蒟蒻、胡蘿蔔及 **1** 料拌炒後，再入高湯續煮１５分鐘即為麵湯。

4 麵條置於碗中，再淋上麵湯即可。

■ 紅燒牛筋刀削麵：將熟陽春麵改為熟刀削麵，其餘材料及做法同紅燒牛筋麵。

880g.(2lb.) ------------------------------boiled plain noodle
400g.(14oz.) ----------------------------boiled beef tendon
200g.(7oz.) --------------------------------bamboo shoot
180g.(6⅓oz.) ------------------------------white yam cake
160g.(5³⁄₅oz.) -----------------------------baby cabbage
60g.(2⅑oz.) --carrot
8½C. --stock
1½T. ----------------------------------minced red shallot
1T. ---minced garlic

■
- •5 sections green onion
- •2 slices ginger
- •4T.soy sauce
- •2T.soy bean paste
- •1T.each hot soy bean paste, sesame oil
- •2t.each red fermented wine rice, sugar
- •¼t.pepper

1 Cut beef tendon into 5 x 2 cm long strips. Cut white yam cake into 2 x 5 cm slices and score diagonal slits on the surface. Wash cabbage clean and cut into 5 cm sections.

2 Wash carrot clean and cut into 2 x 4 cm slices, bamboo into 4 cm sections; scald both in boiling water.

3 Heat the wok, add 3T. oil and heat to hot; stir fry shollt and garlic until fragrant. Add in beef tendon, bamboo, white yam cake, carrot, and ■ to stir fry evenly. Pour in stock and boil for 15 minutes to be the noodle soup.

4 Place noodle in individual bowls, pour over noodle soup and serve.

■ Beef Tendon Stew Soup Shaved Noodle : Replace boiled plain noodle with boiled shaved noodle. The rest of materials and methods are the same as above.

沙嗲牛肉麵

•*Satay Beef Soup Noodle*

四人份 **serve 4**

沙嗲牛肉麵 • *Satay Beef Soup Noodle*

熟陽春麵 ------------ ８８０公克
牛里肌肉 ------------ ３００公克
青江菜 -------------- ２００公克
紅蔥頭 --------------- ４０公克
紅辣椒 --------------- ２０公克
高湯 ------------------- ８杯
蒜末 --------------- ２½大匙
薑末 --------------- １½大匙
太白粉 --------------- １大匙

1
紅豆腐乳 ------------ ２塊
沙茶醬 ------------- ８大匙
椰漿 --------------- ６大匙
紹興酒、咖哩粉、花生醬
、醬油 ---------- 各４大匙
糖 ----------------- ２大匙
蠔油 --------------- １大匙
檸檬皮末、味精 各½小匙

1 牛里肌肉切６×７公分薄片，入油及太白粉各１大匙醃１小時，
紅蔥頭洗淨切末，紅辣椒切小圓圈，青江菜洗淨切段。

2 鍋熱入油４大匙燒熱，入紅蔥頭、紅辣椒、蒜、薑末略炒，再入
1 料拌炒均勻後，入高湯煮開，最後加入牛肉片及青江菜煮熟，
倒入置有麵條的碗中即可。

■ 沙嗲牛肉刀削麵：將熟陽春麵改為熟刀削麵，其餘材料及做法同
沙嗲牛肉麵。

880g.(2lb.)	boiled plain noodle
300g.(10½oz.)	beef fillet
200g.(7oz.)	bok choy
40g.(1$^{2}/_{5}$oz.)	red shallot
20g.($^{2}/_{3}$oz.)	red pepper
8C.	stock
2½T.	minced garlic
1½T.	minced ginger
1T.	corn starch

1
- •2 pieces preserved red bean curd
- •8T.sha-cha paste
- •6T.coconut cream
- •4T.each Chinese shao-shin wine,
  curry powder,peanut paste, soy sauce
- •2T.sugar
- •1T.oyster sauce
- •½t.minced fresh lemon peel

1 Cut beef fillet into 6 x 7 cm thin slices, marinate with
1T. each oil and corn starch for one hour. Wash
shallot clean and mince. Snip red pepper into small
rings. Wash bok choy clean and cut into serving
sections.

2 Heat the wok, add 4T. oil and heat to hot. Stir fry
shallot, red pepper, garlic, and ginger until fragrant.
Add in **1** to fry until evenly mixed. Pour in stock and
bring to boil. Add in beef slices and bok choy to boil
until cooked. Pour over individual bowls of noodle
and serve.

■ Satay Beef Soup Shaved Noodle : Replace boiled plain
noodle with boiled shaved noodle. The rest of
materials and methods are the same as above.

牛肉鍋燒麵 · *Beef Soup Udon in Pot*

烏龍麵 ----------- 880公克	
老豆腐 ----------- 400公克	
番茄 ------------- 350公克	**1** 蛋白 --------------- ½個 醬油、麻油、太白粉 ----- 　　　　　　　　 各1小匙 味精 --------------- ¼小匙 鹽、胡椒粉 ----- 各⅛小匙
牛里肌肉 --------- 200公克	
荷蒿（或青江菜） 160公克	
熟草菇 ----------- 120公克	
魚丸 ------------- 80公克	**2** 鹽、蠔油 ------- 各1小匙 味精、糖、麻油、酒 ----- 　　　　　　　　 各½小匙 胡椒粉 ------------- ⅛小匙
高湯 ------------- 9杯	
蔥段 ------------- 10段	

1 將牛里肌肉切8×4公分薄片，以 **1** 料醃30分鐘，番茄、豆腐均切小塊，豆腐川燙，魚丸對切，荷蒿洗淨備用。
2 鍋熱入油3大匙燒熱，入蔥、番茄炒香後，移入砂鍋並加高湯煮沸，再入烏龍麵、草菇、豆腐、魚丸及 **2** 料煮開，續入荷蒿及牛肉片，再煮開即可。

880g.(2lb.) ----------- udon	
400g.(14oz.) --- bean curd	**1** •½ egg white •1t.each corn starch, soy sauce, sesame oil •⅛t.each salt, pepper
350g.(12⅓oz.) ---- tomato	
200g.(7oz.) ----- beef fillet	
160g.(5⅗oz.) ------------- crown daisy (or bok choy)	
120g.(4¼oz.) ------ canned straw mushroom	**2** •1t.each salt, oyster sauce •½t.each sesame oil, sugar, cooking wine •⅛t.pepper
80g.(2⅘oz.) ------- fish ball	
9C. ------------------- stock	
10 sections -- green onion	

1 Cut beef into 8 x 4 cm thin slices, marinate in **1** for 30 minutes. Cut tomato and bean curd into small cubes. Scald bean curd in boiling water. Cut fish ball into halves. Wash clean crown daisy.
2 Heat the wok, add 3T. oil and heat to hot; stir fry green onion and tomato until fragrant, remove to a ceramic pot. Pour in stock and bring to boil. Add in udon, straw mushroom, bean curd, fish ball, and **2**; bring to boil again. Add in crown daisy and beef, bring to boil once more and serve from the pot.

柱侯牛腩麵 · *Chee Ho Sauce and Beef Soup Noodle*

熟陽春麵 ----------- ８８０公克
牛腩 ----------------- ４００公克
青江菜 ------------- ３００公克
蒜片 ------------------- ２０公克
高湯 --------------------- ８杯
蔥段 ------------------- １０段
蔥末 --------------------- ５大匙
紅蔥頭末、醬油 ------ 各２大匙
薑片 --------------------- ２片

1 ┌ 紅豆腐乳 ------------- ３塊
　　│ 甜麵醬、豆瓣醬、醬油、
　　└ 酒 ----------------- 各２大匙

2 ┌ 麻油 ----------------- １小匙
　　│ 味精、糖 --------- 各¼小匙
　　└ 胡椒粉 ------------- ⅛小匙

1 青江菜一葉葉洗淨，牛腩洗淨切２·５×４·５公分條狀，以２大匙醬油拌勻，鍋熱入油３杯燒至八分熱（１８０℃），入牛腩炸至肉色轉焦黃撈起瀝油。

2 鍋內留油１大匙燒熱，入蔥段、薑片、蒜片爆香，再入牛腩、高湯２杯及 **1** 料煮開，移入燉盅內，入鍋大火蒸１½小時備用。

3 另鍋熱入油２大匙燒熱，將紅蔥頭末爆香，入高湯６杯、**2** 料及蒸好之牛肉湯煮沸，再入青江菜煮熟即為麵湯。

4 麵條置於碗中，灑上蔥末並淋上麵湯即可。

■ 柱侯牛腩刀削麵：將熟陽春麵改為熟刀削麵，其餘材料及做法同柱侯牛腩麵。

880g.(2lb.) --- boiled plain noodle
400g.(14oz.) - beef brisket
300g.(10½oz.) -- bok choy
20g.(⅔oz.) ---- garlic slices
8C. --------------------- stock
10 sections -- green onion
5T. -- minced green onion
2T.each ------- minced red shallot, soy sauce
2 slices -------------- ginger

1 ┌ •3 pieces preserved red bean curd
　　│ •2T.each sweet soy bean paste, soy bean paste, soy sauce, cooking wine

2 ┌ •1t.sesame oil
　　│ •¼t.sugar
　　└ •⅛t.pepper

1 Wash bok choy clean leaf by leaf. Wash beef clean and cut into 2.5 x 4.5 cm strips, mix well with 2T. soy sauce. Heat the wok, add 3C. oil and heat to 180°C (356°F); fry beef until turns dark brown. Drain.

2 Keep 1T. oil in the wok and heat to hot, stir fry green onion sections, ginger slices, and garlic until fragrant. Add in beef, 2C. stock, and **1**; bring to boil, remove into a steam pot. Steam over high heat for 1½ hour.

3 Heat the wok, add 2T. oil and heat to hot; stir fry shallot until fragant. Add in 6C. stock, **2**, and steamed beef soup; bring to boil. Add in bok choy, boil until cooked to be the noodle soup.

4 Place noodle in individual bowls, sprinkle on minced green onions. Pour noodle soup over and serve.

■ Chee Ho Sauce and Beef Soup Shaved Noodle : Replace boiled plain noodle with boiled shaved noodle. The rest of materials and methods are the same as above.

蒜燒小排麵

.Garlic Rib Soup Noodle

四人份　　**serve　4**

蒜燒小排麵 • *Garlic Rib Soup Noodle*

880g.(2lb.)	boiled plain noodle
350g.(12⅓oz.)	baby pork rib
240g.(8²/₅oz.)	bok choy
7½C.	stock
5T.each	minced green onion, minced garlic

熟陽春麵 ----------- ８８０公克
小排骨 ------------- ３５０公克
青江菜 ------------- ２４０公克
高湯 ----------------------- ７½杯
蔥末、蒜末 ----------- 各５大匙

1
- •½ egg white
- •2T.corn starch
- •½T.each minced garlic, minced ginger, soy sauce
- •1t.each sesame oil, cooking wine
- •⅛t.pepper

1
蛋白 -------------------½個
太白粉 ------------- ２大匙
蒜末、薑末、醬油 --------
------------------ 各½大匙
麻油、酒 ------- 各１小匙
味精 ----------------- ¼小匙
胡椒粉 ------------- ⅛小匙

3
醬油 ----------- 1½大匙
麻油 ----------- 1 小匙
鹽 ----------------- ½小匙
味精 ----------------- ¼小匙
胡椒粉 ------------- ⅛小匙

2
- •1C.stock
- •2T.each soy sauce, cooking wine
- •1T.crystal sugar
- •¼t.pepper
- •⅛t.five spices powder

2
高湯 --------------------- 1 杯
醬油、酒 ------- 各２大匙
冰糖 ----------------- 1 大匙
胡椒粉 ------------- ¼小匙
五香粉 ------------- ⅛小匙

3
- •1½T.soy sauce
- •1t.sesame oil
- •½t.salt
- •⅛t.pepper

1 小排骨剁成２．５×２．５公分塊狀，以 **1** 料醃３０分鐘，青江菜洗淨切２公分長段備用。

2 鍋熱入油３大匙燒熱，入蒜末爆香，續入小排骨拌炒，再入**2**料改小火燜煮３０分鐘，其間每隔１０分鐘翻攪一次，待煮透後將小排骨撈起，肉汁留鍋中加入高湯及 **3** 料煮開，入青江菜煮熟即為麵湯。

3 麵條置於碗中，上置小排骨，灑上蔥末，再淋上麵湯即可。

1 Chop pork rib into 2.5 x 2.5 cm square serving pieces, marinate in **1** for 30 minutes. Wash bok choy clean and cut into 2 cm long sections.

2 Heat the wok, add 3T. oil and heat to hot; stir fry minced garlic until fragrant. Stir in ribs to fry, add in **2**; turn heat to low and simmer for 30 minutes, turn the ribs every 10 minutes. When thoroughly cooked, lift out ribs. Keep the juice in the wok, add in stock and **3**, bring to boil. Add in bok choy to boil until cooked. This is the noodle soup.

3 Place noodle in individual bowls, arrange ribs on top, and sprinkle on minced green onion. Pour noodle soup over and serve.

醬味湯麵 • *Soy Bean Flavored Soup Noodle*

熟陽春麵 ----------- ８８０公克	**1**〔 酒 ----------------- ４大匙
絞肉 ---------------- ２００公克	〔 甜麵醬 ------------- ２大匙
小白菜 -------------- １６０公克	〔 味精 ----------------- ¼小匙
高湯 ----------------------- ８杯	
榨菜末 ----------------------²/₃杯	**2**〔 醬油 ----------------- ７大匙
蔥末 ---------------- ２½大匙	〔 芝麻醬 ------------- ６大匙
蒜末 ---------------- ２大匙	〔 烏醋、辣油、麻油
	〔 ------------------ 各1⅓大匙
	〔 味精 ----------------- ½小匙

880g.(2lb.) --- boiled plain noodle
200g.(7oz.) - minced pork
160g.(5³/₅oz.) --------- baby cabbage
8C. ---------------------- stock
²/₃C. -------- minced pickled mustard head
2½T. minced green onion
2T. ---------- minced garlic

1[•4T.cooking wine
[•2T.sweet soy bean paste

2[•7T.soy sauce
[•6T.sesame paste
[•1⅓T.each brown vinegar, chili oil, sesame oil

1 小白菜洗淨切５公分長段備用。

2 鍋熱入油３大匙，入蒜末爆香，再入絞肉炒香，隨即入 **1** 料拌炒均勻盛出。

3 麵條置於碗中，另高湯加 **2** 料及榨菜末煮開，再入小白菜煮熟淋於麵上並灑上蔥末及 **2** 項之材料即可。

■ 醬味刀削湯麵：將熟陽春麵改為熟刀削麵，其餘材料及做法同醬味湯麵。

1 Wash baby cabbage clean and cut into 5 cm long serving sections.

2 Heat the wok, add 3T. oil and heat to hot; stir fry minced garlic until fragrant. Stir in pork to fry, add in **1**; stir fry until evenly mixed. This is the pork sauce.

3 Place noodle in individual bowls. Bring stock to boil with **2** and minced pickled mustard head, then add in baby cabbage to boil until cooked. Pour soup over noodle, sprinkle on minced green onion and pork sauce on top. Serve.

■ Soy Bean Flavored Soup Shaved Noodle : Replace boiled plain noodle with boiled shaved noodle. The rest of materials and methods are the same as above.

雪菜肉絲燜麵 • *Pork and Pickled Green Soup Braised Noodle*

熟陽春麵 ----------- ８８０公克
雪裡紅 -------------- ４００公克
里肌肉 -------------- ３００公克
上湯 ------------------------- ９杯
蔥末、薑末 ----------- 各１大匙

1 ⎡ 太白粉、酒、蛋白 --------
　　 ---------------------- 各２小匙
　　 鹽、味精 --------- 各¼小匙
　　⎣ 胡椒粉 -------------- ⅛小匙

2 ⎡ 麻油、酒、鹽 -- 各１小匙
　　 味精 ------------------- ⅔小匙
　　⎣ 胡椒粉 -------------- ⅛小匙

1 里肌肉切細絲以 **1** 料醃３０分鐘，雪裡紅洗淨切末備用。
2 鍋熱入油４大匙燒熱，入蔥末、肉絲及雪裡紅炒熟，盛起備用。
3 砂鍋內加入上湯煮開，再入麵條煮３分鐘後，續入**2**料、薑末及
　　2 項之材料，再燜煮５分鐘即可。

880g.(2lb.) ---boiled plain noodle
400g.(14oz.) -------pickled mustard green
300g.(10½oz.) - pork fillet
9C. ------------- consommé
1T.each ----minced green onion, minced ginger

1 ⎡ •2t.each corn starch, cooking wine, egg white
　　 •¼t.salt
　　⎣ •⅛t.pepper

2 ⎡ •1t.each sesame oil, cooking wine, salt
　　⎣ •⅛t.pepper

1 Shred pork and marinate in **1** for 30 minutes. Wash pickled mustard green clean and chop fine.
2 Heat the wok, add 4T. oil and heat to hot. Stir fry minced green onion, pork, and pickled mustard green until cooked. Remove.
3 In a ceramic pot, bring consommé to boil; add in noodle to simmer for 3 minutes. Then add in **2**, minced ginger, and pork with pickled mustard green. Simmer for 5 minutes. Serve directly from the pot.

酥肉湯麵 • *Fried Pork Fillet Soup Noodle*

熟陽春麵 ---------- ８８０公克		
里肌肉 ------------ ２４０公克		
海帶芽（泡開）--- １２０公克		
筍片 -------------- ８０公克		
香菇 -------------- １０公克		
高湯 -------------- ８杯		
太白粉 ------------ ４大匙		

❶
醬油 ------------ ２小匙
酒 -------------- １小匙
鹽、味精 ------- 各½小匙
胡椒粉 ---------- ¼小匙

❷
鹽 -------------- ２小匙
酒 -------------- １小匙
味精 ------------ ½小匙
胡椒粉 ---------- ¼小匙

❸
太白粉 ---------- ２杯
蛋 -------------- ４個

1. 里肌肉拍鬆切成１‧５公分寬的條狀，入 ❶ 料醃３０分鐘，再灑上太白粉拌勻，香菇泡軟去蒂切片，海帶芽切８公分條狀。
2. ❸ 料拌勻成麵糊，鍋熱入油３杯燒至七分熱（１６０℃），肉條裹上麵糊入鍋炸至金黃色撈起。
3. 高湯煮開，加入香菇、筍、海帶芽及 ❷ 料煮１０分鐘，再入炸好的肉條續煮約４分鐘即為酥肉湯。
4. 麵條置於碗中，再淋上酥肉湯即可。

880g.(2lb.) ---boiled plain noodle
240g.(8²⁄₅oz.) ---pork fillet
120g.(4¼oz.) ----seaweed sprout (soaked)
80g.(2⁴⁄₅oz.) ------bamboo shoot slices
10g.(⅓oz.) -----dried black mushroom
8C. ---------------------stock
4T. -------------corn starch

❶
- 2t.soy sacue
- 1t.cooking wine
- ½t.salt
- ¼t.pepper

❷
- 2t.salt
- 1t.cooking wine
- ¼t.pepper

❸
- 2C.corn starch
- 4 eggs

1. Loosen pork fillet with the back of a knife and cut into 1.5 cm wide strips, marinate in **❶** for 30 minutes; dust with corn starch and coat evenly. Soften mushroom in warm water, discard stem, and slice. Cut seaweed sprout into 8 cm long strips.
2. Mix **❸** evenly into a batter. Heat the wok, add 3C. oil and heat to 160°C (320°F). Roll pork strips in the batter and deep fry until golden.
3. Bring stock to boil, add in mushroom, bamboo, seaweed sprout, and **❷**; simmer for 10 minutes. Add in fried pork and continue simmer for 4 minutes to be the fried pork soup.
4. Place noodle in individual bowls, pour fried pork soup over and serve.

嫩雞煨麵 · *Chicken Soup Braised Noodle*

熟陽春麵	880公克	熟筍	100公克
雞腿	360公克	蝦米	20公克
菠菜	240公克	高湯	10杯
菜心	200公克	蔥段	12段

❶
- 鹽 ----------------- 1½小匙
- 麻油 --------------- 1小匙
- 味精、糖 --------- 各½小匙
- 胡椒粉 ------------- ¼小匙

1 雞腿剁成3×3公分小塊，入鍋川燙撈起瀝乾，菜心、熟筍均切5×1公分長條狀，菠菜洗淨切5公分段備用。

2 鍋熱入油3大匙燒熱，入蔥段、蝦米爆香，續入菜心、熟筍略炒後，盛起備用。

3 鍋內加入高湯及雞腿煮開，再入麵條煮3分鐘後，續入 **❶** 料及 **2** 項之材料，再煨煮5分鐘即可。

880g.(2lb.) ---boiled plain noodle
360g.(12²/₃oz.)chicken leg
240g.(8²/₅oz.) -----spinach
200g.(7oz.) --------- peeled mustard stick

100g.(3½oz.) ------ canned bamboo shoot
20g.(²/₃oz.) ----- dried baby shrimp
10C. -------------------- stock
12 sections -- green onion

❶
- 1½t.salt
- 1t.sesame oil
- ½t.sugar
- ¼t.pepper

1 Chop chicken leg into 3 x 3 cm serving pieces, parboil in boiling water, drain. Cut mustard stick and bamboo into 5 x 1 cm long strips. Wash spinach clean and cut into 5 cm long sections.

2 Heat the wok, add 3T. oil and heat to hot; stir fry green onion and dried shrimp until fragrant. Add into mustard stick and bamboo to fry for a while.

3 Pour stock and chicken into a ceramic pot, bring to boil over high heat. Add in noodle cook for 3 minutes, season with **❶** and rest of the materials simmer for 5 minutes. Serve directly from the pot.

片兒川麵 · *Hangzhou Style Pork Soup Noodle*

熟陽春麵 ----------- ８００公克	
里肌肉 ------------- ２８０公克	
草菇 -------------- １８０公克	
酸菜、韭黃 ----- 各１４０公克	
熟筍 -------------- １００公克	
上湯 ------------------- ８杯	

1
- 醬油 ------------- 1 小匙
- 太白粉 ---------- ½小匙
- 糖 --------------- ¼小匙

2
- 酒、油 -------- 各２小匙
- 鹽 --------------- 1 小匙
- 糖、味精 ------- 各½小匙
- 胡椒粉 ---------- ⅛小匙

1 里肌肉切３×４公分薄片，以 **1** 料醃３０分鐘後蒸熟備用。
2 草菇、筍均切薄片，韭黃切段，酸菜洗淨切末。
3 鍋熱入豬油３大匙燒熱，入酸菜末略炒，再入草菇、筍及上湯煮開，再以 **2** 料調味並加麵條煮至入味後，再入韭黃及肉片即可。
■ 酸菜及韭黃可以雪裡紅取代。

880g.(2lb.) --- boiled plain noodle
280g.(9⅘oz.) --- pork fillet
180g.(6⅓oz.) -------- straw mushroom
140g.(5oz.)each ------ sour mustard, yellow chive
100g.(3½oz.) ------ canned bamboo shoot
8C. ------------ consommé

1
- 1t.soy sauce
- ½t.corn starch
- ¼t.sugar

2
- 2t.each cooking wine, sesame oil
- 1t.salt
- ½t.sugar
- ⅛t.pepper

1 Cut pork fillet into 3 x 4 cm thin slices, marinate in **1** for 30 minutes. Steamed until cooked.
2 Cut straw mushroom and bamboo into thin slices, chive into sections. Wash sour mustard clean and chop fine.
3 Heat the wok, add 3T. oil and heat to hot. Stir fry sour mustard slightly, add in starw mushroom, bamboo, and consommé; bring to boil, season with **2**. Add in noodle and simmer until tasty. Stir in chive and pork. Serve.
■ Sour mustard and yellow chive can be replace by pickled mustard green.

番茄刀削麵・*Tomato Soup Shaved Noodle*

紅番茄 ----------- 3100公克	高湯 ------------------------- 9杯		
熟刀削麵 ----------- 800公克	蔥末 ------------------------- 5大匙		
絞肉 -------------------- 400公克	蒜末 ------------------------- 1大匙		
小白菜 ------------------ 240公克	薑末 ------------------------⅓大匙		

1
```
糖 -------------------- 2小匙
鹽 -------------------- 1小匙
味精 ----------------- ½小匙
胡椒粉 --------------- ⅛小匙
```

1 番茄去皮去籽切1．5公分塊狀，小白菜洗淨切段備用。

2 鍋熱入油5大匙燒熱，入蒜、薑末爆香後，再入絞肉拌炒，改小火炒至肉色轉黑且酥後撈起，鍋剩油將番茄炒勻（約5分鐘）後，入絞肉拌炒，再入高湯及 **1** 料，以小火燜煮約1小時後，入小白菜煮開即為麵湯。

3 麵條置於碗中，灑上蔥末，再淋上麵湯即可。

■ 番茄麵片湯、番茄湯麵：將熟刀削麵改為熟麵片或熟陽春麵，其餘材料及做法同番茄刀削麵。

3100g.(6⁴/₅lb.) red tomato
880g.(2lb.) ---------- boiled shaved noodle
400g.(14oz.) minced pork
240g.(8²/₅oz.) --------- baby cabbage

9C. --------------------- stock
5T. -- minced green onion
1T. ----------- minced garlic
⅓T. -------- minced ginger

1
```
•2t.sugar
•1t.salt
•⅛t.pepper
```

1 Peel skin off tomato, discard seeds, and cut into 1.5 cm cubes. Wash baby cabbage clean and cut into serving sections.

2 Heat the wok, add 5T. oil and heat to hot; stir fry garlic and ginger until fragrant. Add in minced pork to fry, turn heat low and fry until color darkened and crispy, remove. With the remaining oil in the wok, stir fry tomato (about 5 minutes), add in pork and mix evenly. Pour in stock and **1**, simmer over low heat for one hour. Add in baby cabbage and bring to boil again. This is the tomato noodle soup.

3 Place noodle in individual bowls, sprinkle on minced green onion. Pour tomato noodle soup over the noodle and serve.

■ Tomato Soup Noodle Pieces and Tomato Soup Noodle: Replace boiled shaved noodle with boiled noodle pieces or boiled plain noodle. The rest of materials and methods are the same as above.

鳳梨苦瓜雞麵 • *Tropical Chicken Soup Noodle String*

熟白麵線 ---------- 8 8 0公克		高湯 ------------------------ 8杯		
味噌 ----------------- 2 5 0公克				

❶
- 雞肉 ---------- 8 0 0公克
- 苦瓜 ---------- 4 0 0公克
- 鳳梨淨重 ----- 3 0 0公克

❷
- 酒 ----------------- 3大匙
- 冰糖、麻油 -- 各1½大匙
- 味精 ---------------- ¼小匙

1 雞肉洗淨剁4×3公分塊狀,苦瓜去籽洗淨與鳳梨均切3×3公分塊狀,將雞肉與苦瓜入開水川燙瀝乾備用。
2 高湯與味噌調勻並煮開,再入❶、❷料續煮1 0分鐘即為麵湯。
3 麵線置於碗中,淋上麵湯即可。

880g.(2lb.) -- boiled white noodle string
250g.(8⁴/₅oz.) --------- miso
8C. --------------------stock

❶
- 3T.cooking wine
- 1½T.each crystal sugar, sesame oil

❷
- 800g.(1¾lb.) chicken breast
- 400g.(14oz.) bitter melon
- 300g.(10½oz.) pineapple(net weight)

1 Wash chicken clean and cut into 4 x 3 cm cubes. Discard seeds in bitter melon and rinse clean; cut with pineapple into 3 x 3 cm cubes. Parboil both chicken and bitter melon in boiling water and drain.
2 Mix stock and miso well, bring to boil. Add in ❶ and ❷, continue boiling for 10 minutes to be the noodle soup.
3 Place noodle string in individual bowls, pour over noodle soup and serve.

四人份　**serve 4**

原盅蔘雞麵 • *Steamed Ginseng Chicken Soup Noodle*

熟陽春麵 ----------- 8 8 0公克
雞腿 ----------------- 8 2 0公克
西洋蔘 -------------- 1 0公克

❶
- 鹽 ----------------- 2小匙
- 味精 ---------------- ¼小匙

1 雞腿洗淨剁3×4公分塊狀,入燉盅內加水8杯及西洋蔘大火蒸約1小時,至雞肉熟爛再加❶料調味即為蔘雞湯。
2 麵條置於碗中,淋上蔘雞湯即可。

880g.(2lb.) --- boiled plain noodle
820g.(1⁴/₅lb.) - chicken leg

10g.(⅓oz.) ------ American ginseng
2t. ----------------------- salt

1 Wash chicken clean and chop into 3 x 4 cm serving pieces. Place chicken in a ceramic steam pot, add 8C. water, and ginseng; steam over high heat for one hour until chicken is tender. Season with salt.
2 Place noodle in individual bowls, pour ginseng chicken soup over and serve.

斑球兩面黃 · *Fish Fillet on Noodle Pancake*

兩面黃 -------------- ６８０公克	熟筍 ------------------ １４０公克
魚肉、油菜------各２４０公克	

1
- 香菇 ------------- １６公克
- 蔥段 ------------- ２０段
- 薑片 ------------- ４片

3
- 高湯 -------------------- ２杯
- 醬油 -------------------- ２大匙
- 太白粉 -------------- １大匙
- 糖 ----------------------- １小匙
- 鹽、味精 ---------- 各¼小匙

2
- 油 ----------------------- ２大匙
- 鹽 ----------------------- ½小匙
- 胡椒粉 --------------- ¼小匙

1 在魚肉內面劃上深度的菱形花紋後，再切成２×４公分片狀，入 **2**料拌醃，香菇泡軟去蒂切１公分條狀，筍切１×４×０‧２公分片狀，油菜洗淨切段備用。

2 鍋熱入油４杯燒至五分熱（１２０℃），入魚片過油至變色，隨即撈起瀝油。

3 鍋內留油２大匙燒熱，入 **1**料爆香，續入油菜、熟筍拌炒均勻，再入 **3** 料、魚片煮開，淋於兩面黃上即可。

680g.(1½lb.) ------ noodle pancake
240g.(8²/₅oz.)each ----fish fillet, rape or other greens

140g.(5oz.) --------canned bamboo shoot

1
- 16g.(³/₅oz.) dried black mushroom
- 20 sections green onion
- 4 slices ginger

3
- 2C.stock
- 2T.soy sauce
- 1T.corn starch
- 1t.sugar
- ¼t.salt

2
- 2T.oil
- ½t.salt
- ¼t.pepper

1 Score diagonal diamond slits on the inner surface of fish fillet, then cut into 2 x 4 cm slices; marinate in **2**. Soften mushroom in warm water, discard stem and julienne into 1 cm strips. Cut bamboo into 1 x 4 x 0.2 cm slices. Wash rape clean and cut into serving sections.

2 Heat the wok, add 4C. oil and heat to 120°C (248°F). Soak fish fillet in hot oil until color turns pale, lift out and drain.

3 Keep 2T. oil in the wok and heat to hot, stir fry **1** until fragrant. Add in rape and bamboo, mix evenly; then add in **3** and fish fillet, bring to boil. Pour over noodle and serve.

鐵板蝦仁麵

.Shrimp Noodle on Sizzling Platter

四人份　　serve　4

鐵板蝦仁麵 · *Shrimp Noodle on Sizzling Platter*

兩面黃 -------------	680公克
蝦仁、大白菜 --- 各200公克
瘦肉 --------------	160公克
青花菜 ------------	120公克
洋蔥、熟筍 ------ 各100公克
胡蘿蔔 ------------	60公克
薑片 --------------	6片

1
蛋白 --------------	½個
太白粉 -----------	1⅓大匙
酒 ---------------	2小匙
鹽 ---------------	¼小匙
胡椒粉 -----------	⅛小匙

3
高湯 --------------	3杯
醬油 --------------	2大匙
太白粉 -----------	2小匙
麻油、酒 -------	各1小匙
鹽、味精、胡椒粉 -------
--------------------	各½小匙

2
油 ---------------	2大匙
酒 ---------------	2小匙
醬油 --------------	1小匙
鹽 ---------------	¼小匙
胡椒粉 -----------	⅛小匙

1 蝦仁去腸泥洗淨，入 **1** 料拌醃，瘦肉切1×4公分之薄片，以 **2** 料拌醃，大白菜、洋蔥、胡蘿蔔、筍洗淨，切3×1公分之片狀，青花菜切小朵。

2 鍋熱入油3杯燒至五分熱（120℃）將蝦仁、瘦肉入鍋過油至變色，隨即撈起，再入胡蘿蔔、筍片、青花菜過油，隨即撈起瀝油。

3 鐵板燒熱，入兩面黃備用。

4 鍋內留油3大匙燒熱，依次入薑片、洋蔥、大白菜拌炒，續入 **3** 料及 **2** 項之材料煮開，再淋於鐵板之兩面黃上即可。

680g.(1½lb.) ----------------------------- noodle pancake
200g.(7oz.)each ------- shelled shrimp, Chinese cabbage
160g.(5⅗oz.) ----------------------------------- lean pork
120g.(4¼oz.) ------------------------------------ broccoli
100g.(3½oz.)each -------- onion, canned bamboo shoot
60g.(2⅑oz.) --------------------------------------- carrot
6 slices --- ginger

1
- ½ egg white
- 1⅓T.corn starch
- 2t.cooking wine
- ¼t.salt
- ⅛t.pepper

2
- 2T.oil
- 2t.cooking wine
- 1t.soy sauce
- ¼t.salt
- ⅛t.pepper

3
- 3C.stock
- 2T.soy sauce
- 2t.corn starch
- 1t.each sesame oil, cooking wine
- ½t.each salt, pepper

1 Devein shrimp and wash clean, marinate in **1**. Cut pork into 1 x 4 cm thin slices, marinate in **2**. Wash cabbage, onion, carrot, and bamboo clean; cut all into 3 x 1 cm serving pieces. Snip broccoli into small sprigs.

2 Heat the wok, add 3C. oil and heat to 120℃ (248℉). Soak shrimp and pork in oil until color turns pale, lift out. Add carrot, bamboo, and broccoli into oil, lift out immediately.

3 Heat the sizzling platter, place noodle on.

4 Keep 3T. oil in the wok,stir in by order of ginger, onion, and cabbage to fry; then add in **3** and materials of **2**. Bring to boil, and pour over the noodle. Serve.

干燒蝦仁伊麵 · *Shrimp E-Fu Noodle*

伊麵 ----------------- ３６０公克	熟青豆仁 ----------- １５０公克
蝦仁 ----------------- ３００公克	

1
[蔥末 ---------------- ２½大匙
[蒜末 ---------------- ２大匙
[薑末 ---------------- １½大匙

2
[蛋白 ---------------- ½個
[太白粉 ------------- １大匙
[鹽 ------------------ ¼小匙

3
[高湯 ---------------- ４杯
[番茄醬 ------------- ３大匙
[醬油 ---------------- ２大匙
[酒釀、糖 -------- 各１大匙
[辣豆瓣醬 ---------- １小匙
[鹽 ------------------ ¼小匙

4
[水 ------------------ ２大匙
[太白粉 ------------- １⅓大匙

1 蝦仁去腸泥洗淨，入 **2** 料拌醃備用。
2 鍋熱入油３杯燒至五分熱（１２０℃），入蝦仁過油至變色即撈起瀝油。
3 鍋內留油２大匙燒熱，入 **1** 料爆香，續入 **3** 料煮開，再入蝦仁及青豆仁煮約３分鐘，以 **4** 料勾芡，淋於伊麵上即可。

360g.(12²/₃oz.)e-fu noodle
300g.(10½oz.)-----shelled shrimp

150g.(5⅓oz.) -------boiled green peas

1
•2½T.minced green onion
•2T.minced gralic
•1½T.minced ginger

2
•½ egg white
•1T.corn starch
•¼t.salt

3
•4C.stock
•3T.tomato catchup
•2T.soy sauce
•1T.each fermented wine rice, sugar
•1t.hot soy bean paste
•¼t.salt

4
•2T.water
•1⅓T.corn starch

1 Devein shrimp and wash clean, marinate in **2**.
2 Heat the wok, add 3C. oil and heat to 120℃ (248°F). Soak shrimp in oil until color turns pale, lift out.
3 Keep 2T. oil in the wok and heat to hot; stir fry **1** until fragrant. Add in **3** and bring to boil, stir in shrimp and green peas; simmer for 3 minutes. Thicken with **4**, pour over noodle and serve.

番茄蝦仁麵・*Tomato and Shrimp Noodle*

兩面黃 -------------- ６８０公克	番茄醬 -------------------- ３大匙
紅番茄 -------------- ３００公克	

1
- 蝦仁 ---------- １６０公克
- 洋蔥 ---------- １２０公克
- 四季豆 ---------- ４０公克

2
- 蛋白 ------------------ ½個
- 太白粉 ---------- １⅓大匙
- 酒 ------------------ ２小匙
- 鹽、胡椒粉 ----- 各¼小匙

3
- 高湯 ------------------ ２杯
- 酒 ------------------ ２小匙
- 糖 ------------------ １小匙
- 鹽 ------------------ ⅔小匙
- 味精 ---------------- ½小匙
- 胡椒粉 ------------- ¼小匙

4
- 水 ------------------ ２大匙
- 太白粉 ------------- ２小匙

1 蝦仁去腸泥洗淨，入 **2** 料拌醃備用。
2 番茄去皮、去籽，切１・５公分小塊，四季豆去老纖維洗淨，與洋蔥均切１・５公分小片。
3 鍋熱入油３大匙燒熱，入 **1** 料炒熟撈起備用。
4 鍋內續入油２大匙燒熱，先入番茄炒香，再入番茄醬炒拌均勻後，續入 **1**、**3** 料煮開，再以 **4** 料芶芡，淋於兩面黃上即可。

680g.(1½lb.) ------- noodle pancake	300g.(10½oz.) ---- tomato 3T. ------- tomato catchup

1
- •160g.(5³/₅oz.)shelled shrimp
- •120g.(4¼oz.)onion
- •40g.(1²/₅oz.)string bean

2
- •½ egg white
- •1⅓T.corn starch
- •2t.cooking wine
- •¼t.each salt, pepper

3
- •2C.stock
- •2t.cooking wine
- •1t.sugar
- •⅔t.salt
- •¼t.pepper

4
- •2T.water
- •2t.corn starch

1 Devein shrimp and wash clean, marinate in **2**.
2 Skin tomato, discard seeds, and cut into 1.5 cm cubes. Peel off tough fibers of string bean and wash clean, cut the same as onion into 1.5 cm small pieces.
3 Heat the wok, add 3T. oil and heat to hot; stir fry **1** until cooked and remove.
4 Add 2T. oil in the wok and heat to hot; stir fry tomato until fragrant, and add in catchup, mix well. Then add **1** and **3**, bring to boil. Thicken with **4**, pour over noodle and serve.

鮮魷炸麵 • *Squid on Deep Fried Noodle*

青江菜 ------------- 400公克	熟筍、熟洋菇 --- 各140公克	400g.(14oz.) ---- bok choy	•3C.stock
炸麵 --------------- 360公克	蔥段 ------------------ 20段	360g.(12²/₃oz.) ------- deep fried noodle	•2T.each soy sauce, white vinegar
花枝淨重 ---------- 320公克	薑片 ------------------- 4片	320g.(10¼oz.) ------- squid (net weight)	•1⅓T.corn starch

1
- 高湯 ------------------ 3杯
- 醬油、白醋 ----- 各2大匙
- 太白粉 ------------ 1⅓大匙
- 酒、糖 ----------- 各1小匙
- 鹽、味精 -------- 各½小匙

140g.(5oz.)each -- canned bamboo shoot, canned mushroom
20 sections -- green onion
4 slices --------------- ginger

1
- •3C.stock
- •2T.each soy sauce, white vinegar
- •1⅓T.corn starch
- •1t.each cooking wine, sugar
- •½t.salt

1 花枝洗淨切片，青江菜縱切為4份，洋菇切0．2公分薄片，筍切0．2×1×4公分片狀，薑切小片。

2 鍋熱入油4杯燒至五分熱（120℃），入花枝、筍、洋菇過油，隨即撈起瀝油。

3 鍋內留油2大匙燒熱，爆香蔥、薑，再入青江菜炒數下後，續入花枝、筍、洋菇及 **1** 料煮開，再淋於炸麵上即可。

■ 鮮魷伊麵：將炸麵改為伊麵，其餘材料及做法同鮮魷炸麵。

1 Wash squid and cut into serving slices. Quarter bok choy lengthwise. Cut mushroom into 0.2 cm thin slices, bamboo into 0.2 x 1 x 4 cm slices, and ginger into small slices.

2 Heat the wok, add 4C. oil and heat to 120℃ (248°F). Soak squid, bamboo, and mushroom in oil; lift out immediately.

3 Keep 2T. oil in the wok and heat to hot, stir fry green onion and ginger until fragrant. Add in bok choy to fry a while, then stir in squid, bamboo, mushroom, and **1**; bring to boil. Pour over noodle and serve.

■ Squid on E-Fu Noodle : Replace deep fried noodle with e-fu noodle. The rest of materials and methods are the same as above.

豆豉蛤蜊麵 • *Clam Noodle in Black Bean Sauce*

熟陽春麵 ----------- ８８０公克
蛤蜊 --------------- ５００公克
青椒 --------------- ２００公克
紅辣椒 ------------- ３０公克
蔥白 --------------- ２０公克
薑、蒜頭 ---------- 各１５公克

1 ［ 水 -------------------- ²⁄₃杯
　　 酒 -------------------- 2小匙

2 ［ 水 -------------------- 4大匙
　　 酒、豆豉 -------- 各2大匙
　　 醬油 --------------- 1⅓大匙
　　 蠔油、糖、麻油各1小匙
　　 味精、胡椒粉 --- 各½小匙

1 蛤蜊浸鹽水吐沙洗淨，豆豉泡軟剁碎，青椒、紅辣椒去籽切2公分之片狀，蔥白切1．5公分段，薑、蒜頭切小片。
2 鍋熱入油2大匙燒熱，爆香蔥、薑、蒜，續入蛤蜊及 **1** 料拌炒至蛤蜊開口，再依次入 **2** 料、青椒、麵條、紅辣椒拌炒均匀即可。
■ 豆豉蛤蜊刀削麵：將熟陽春麵改為熟刀削麵，其餘材料及做法同豆豉蛤蜊麵。

880g.(2lb.) --- boiled plain noodle
500g.(1¹⁄₁₀lb.) --------- clam
200g.(7oz.) green pepper
30g.(1oz.) ----- red pepper
20g.(²⁄₃oz.) --- green onion (white part only)
15g.(½oz.)each ---- ginger, garlic

1 • ²⁄₃C.water
　　 • 2t.cooking wine

2 • 4T.water
　　 • 2T.each cooking wine, fermented black soy bean
　　 • 1⅓T.soy sauce
　　 • 1t.each oyster sauce, sugar, sesame oil
　　 • ½t.pepper

1 Cover clam with salted water to rid of the sand and rinse clean. Soften black bean in little water and chop fine. Discard seeds in green and red pepper, cut into 2 cm serving slices. Cut white part of green onion into 1.5 cm sections. Cut ginger and garlic into small slices.
2 Heat the wok, add 2T. oil and heat hot; stir fry green onion, ginger, and garlic until fragrant. Stir in clam and **1**, stir fry until clam opens. Then add in by order of **2**, green pepper, noodle, and red pepper; mix well and serve.
■ Clam Shaved Noodle in Black Bean Sauce : Replace boiled plain noodle with boiled shaved noodle. The rest of materials and methods are the same as above.

鮮貝炒麵

. Fresh Scallop Noodle

四人份　**serve　4**

鮮貝炒麵 • *Fresh Scallop Noodle*

熟陽春麵 ----------- ８８０公克
鮮干貝 ------------- ２５０公克
西洋芹 ------------- １００公克
胡蘿蔔 ------------- ９０公克
豌豆莢、濕木耳 --- 各４０公克
蔥段 --------------------- １０段
薑片 ---------------------- ３片
辣豆瓣醬 --------------- ½小匙

1 ┌ 酒 ----------------- ２小匙
   └ 鹽 ----------------- ¼小匙

2 ┌ 水 ------------------- ３大匙
   │ 醬油 --------------- ２²/₃大匙
   │ 酒 ----------------- １¹/₃大匙
   │ 烏醋 --------------- １大匙
   │ 糖 ------------------ １小匙
   │ 味精 --------------- ½小匙
   └ 胡椒粉 ------------- ¼小匙

1 鮮干貝洗淨橫切成０．３公分厚之片狀，入 **1** 料拌醃。
2 胡蘿蔔去皮，切３×１．５×０．２公分薄片，西洋芹去老纖維切斜片，木耳洗淨切３×１．５公分薄片，豌豆莢去老纖維洗淨。
3 鍋熱入油４杯燒至五分熱（１２０c），入鮮貝過油即撈起，再入西洋芹、胡蘿蔔、豌豆莢、木耳過油，隨即撈起備用。
4 鍋內留油２大匙，入蔥段、薑片、辣豆瓣醬爆香，再依次入麵條、西洋芹、胡蘿蔔、豌豆莢、木耳、鮮貝及 **2** 料拌炒均勻即可。
■ 鮮貝刀切麵：將熟陽春麵改為熟刀切麵，其餘材料及做法同鮮貝炒麵。

880g.(2lb.) ------------------------------boiled plain noodle
250g.(8⁴/₅oz.) ------------------------------fresh scallop
100g.(3½oz.) ------------------------------------celery
90g.(3¹/₅oz.) ------------------------------------carrot
40g.(1²/₅oz.)each ----snow pea pod, soaked black wood ear
10 sections --------------------------------green onion
3 slices--ginger
½t. ------------------------------------hot soy bean paste

1 ┌ •2t.cooking wine
   └ •¼t.salt

2 ┌ •3T.water
   │ •2²/₃T.soy sauce
   │ •1¹/₃T.cooking wine
   │ •1T.brown vinegar
   │ •1t.sugar
   └ •¼t.pepper

1 Wash scallop clean and cut widthwise into 0.3 cm thick slices, marinate in **1**.
2 Skin carrot and cut into 3 x 1.5 x 0.2 cm thin slices. Peel off tough fibers on celery and cut into slanting slices. Wash wood ear clean and cut into 3 x 1.5 cm thin slices. Peel off tough fibers on snow pea pod and wash clean.
3 Heat the wok, add 4C. oil and heat to 120°C (248°F). Soak scallop in oil and lift out immediately. Then soak carrot, pea pod, and wood ear in the oil; lift out and drain.
4 Keep 2T. oil in the wok, stir fry green onion, ginger, and soy bean paste until fragrant. Add in by order of noodle, celery. carrot, pea pod, wood ear, scallop, and **2**. Mix well and heat thoroughly, serve.
■ Scallop Handmade Noodle: Replace boiled plain noodle with boiled handmade noodle. The rest of materials and methods are the same as above.

雙鮮炒麵 · *Pork and Shrimp Fried Noodle*

熟雞蛋麵 ------------ ８８０公克	肉絲、蝦仁 ------ 各２００公克
綠豆芽 -------------- ２４０公克	香菜 --------------------- ２０公克

1
- 蔥末 ------------------ ２½大匙
- 蒜末 ------------------ １大匙

2
- 蛋白 ---------------------- １個
- 太白粉、酒 ----各２小匙
- 鹽 ----------------------- ¼小匙

3
- 油 ---------------------- ２大匙
- 醬油 ------------------ ２小匙
- 糖 --------------------- １小匙
- 胡椒粉 ---------------- ¼小匙

4
- 高湯 --------------------- １杯
- 醬油 --------------------- ２大匙
- 麻油 --------------------- ２小匙
- 胡椒粉、味精、鹽 --------
- -------------------- 各¼小匙

1 肉絲入 **3** 料拌醃，蝦仁去腸泥洗淨，入 **2** 料拌醃，綠豆芽洗淨，
香菜洗淨切末備用。
2 鍋熱入油３大匙燒熱，入 **1** 料爆香，續入肉絲、蝦仁炒拌均勻，
再入綠豆芽、麵條及 **4** 料炒勻，最後入香菜拌勻即可。
■ 雙鮮炒麵之熟雞蛋麵可以熟陽春麵取代。

880g.(2lb.) ----boiled egg noodle
240g.(8²/₅oz.) bean sprout

200g.(7oz.)each --shelled shrimp, shredded pork
20g.(²/₃oz.) ------coriander

1
- •2½T.minced green onion
- •1T.minced garlic

3
- •2T.oil
- •2t.soy sauce
- •1t.sugar
- •¼t.pepper

2
- •1 egg white
- •2t.each corn starch, cooking wine
- •¼t.salt

4
- •1C.stock
- •2T.soy sauce
- •2t.sesame oil
- •¼t.each salt, pepper

1 Marinate shredded pork in **3**. Devein shrimp and wash clean, marinate in **2**. Wash bean sprout clean. Wash coriander clean and chop fine.
2 Heat the wok, add 3T. oil and heat to hot. Stir fry **1** until fragrant. Add in pork and shrimp, stir fry evenly. Add in bean sprout, noodle, and **4**; mix well and heat thoroughly. Mix in coriander and serve.
■ Boiled egg noodle can be replaced by boiled plain noodle.

什錦伊麵 · *Mix-Fried E-Fu Noodle*

伊麵 ---------------- 3 6 0 公克	洋火腿 ---------------- 8 0 公克	
小白菜 ------------- 2 0 0 公克	香菇 ---------------------- 8 公克	

1
- 花枝淨重 ----- 1 4 0 公克
- 瘦肉 ---------- 1 2 0 公克
- 熟筍 ---------- 1 0 0 公克
- 蝦仁 ------------- 8 0 公克

3
- 高湯 -------------------- 3 杯
- 醬油、酒 ------- 各 2 大匙
- 鹽 -------------------- ½ 小匙
- 胡椒粉、味精 --- 各¼ 小匙

2
- 油 ------------------- 1 大匙
- 醬油、酒 ---------- 各½ 小匙
- 糖 ------------------- ¼ 小匙
- 鹽、胡椒粉 ------ 各⅛ 小匙

4
- 水 ------------------- 2 大匙
- 太白粉 ----------- 1 ⅓ 大匙

1 花枝洗淨切片，蝦仁去腸泥洗淨，瘦肉、洋火腿、熟筍均切 3 × 1 公分片狀，肉片入 **2** 料拌醃，香菇泡軟去蒂對切，小白菜洗淨切段。

2 鍋熱入油 4 杯燒至五分熱（1 2 0℃），將花枝、蝦仁、肉片入鍋過油至變色，隨即撈起瀝油備用。

3 鍋內留油 2 大匙燒熱，將香菇、火腿炒香，續入 **1** 料、**3** 料及小白菜煮開，再以 **4** 料芶芡，淋於伊麵上即可

360g.(12⅔oz.)e-fu noodle
200g.(7oz.) baby cabbage
80g.(2⅘oz.) - virginia ham

8g.(¼oz.) ------ dried black mushroom

1
- •140g.(5oz.) squid (net weight)
- •120g.(4¼oz.) lean pork
- •100g.(3½oz.) canned bamboo shoot
- •80g.(2⅘oz.) shelled shrimp

2
- •1T.oil
- •½t.each soy sauce, cooking wine
- •¼t.sugar
- •⅛t.each pepper, salt

4
- •2T.water
- •1⅓T.corn starch

3
- •3C.stock
- •2T.each soy sauce, cooking wine
- •½t.salt
- •¼t.pepper

1 Wash squid clean and cut into serving slices. Devein shrimp and rinse clean. Cut pork, ham, and bamboo all into 3 x 1 cm slices. Marinate pork in **2**. Soften mushroom in warm water, discard stem, and cut into halves. Wash baby cabbage clean and cut into serving sections.

2 Heat the wok, add 4C. oil and heat to 120°C (248°F). Soak squid, shrimp, and pork in oil until colors turn pale. Lift out immediately and drain.

3 Keep 2T. oil in the wok and heat to hot, stir fry mushroom and ham until fragrant. Add in **1**, **3**, and cabbage; bring to boil. Thicken with **4**, pour over noodle and serve.

沙茶牛柳伊麵 · *Sha-Cha Beef E-Fu Noodle*

| 伊麵 | 360公克 | 牛肉 | 240公克 |

伊麵 ----------------- 360公克 　　牛肉 ----------------- 240公克
芥藍菜 -------------- 300公克

1 ┌ 沙茶醬 ------------ 3大匙
　　└ 蒜末 --------------- 1大匙

2 ┌ 水 ----------------- 4大匙
　　│ 油 ----------------- 2大匙
　　│ 醬油 -------------- 1大匙
　　│ 太白粉 ----------- 2小匙
　　└ 小蘇打、胡椒粉 各¼小匙

3 ┌ 高湯 ----------------- 3杯
　　│ 醬油、太白粉 各1⅓大匙
　　│ 糖 --------------------- 1小匙
　　│ 鹽 --------------------- ½小匙
　　└ 胡椒粉 -------------- ¼小匙

1 牛肉切5×1公分薄片，入 **2** 料拌醃，芥藍菜洗淨切3公分長段。

2 鍋熱入油4杯燒至五分熱（120℃），入牛肉過油至變色，隨即撈起瀝油。

3 鍋內留油2大匙燒熱，入芥藍菜炒熟撈起，再入 **1** 料爆香，續入 **3** 料煮開，再入牛肉、芥藍菜煮開，淋於伊麵上即可。

■ 沙茶牛柳炸麵：將伊麵改為炸麵，其餘材料及做法同沙茶牛柳伊麵。

360g.(12⅔oz.) -------- e-fu noodle　　300g.(10½oz.) ------ gailan
240g.(8⅖oz.) --------- beef

1 • 3T.sha-cha paste
　　• 1T.minced garlic

2 • 4T.water
　　• 2T.oil
　　• 1T.soy sauce
　　• 2t.corn starch
　　• ¼t.each baking soda, pepper

3 • 3C.stock
　　• 1⅓T.each soy sauce, corn starch
　　• 1t.sugar
　　• ½t.salt
　　• ¼t.pepper

1 Cut beef into 5 x 1 cm thin slices, marinate in **2**. Wash gailan clean and cut into 3 cm long serving sections.

2 Heat the wok, add 4C. oil and heat to 120°C (248°F). Soak beef in oil until color turns pale, lift out and drain.

3 Keep 2T. oil in the wok, stir fry gailan until cooked; remove. Stir fry **1** until fragrant, add in **3** and bring to boil. Then stir in beef and gailan. Mix well and heat thouroughly, pour over noodle and serve.

■ Sha-Cha Beef on Deep Fried Noodle : Replace e-fu noodle with deep fried noodle. The rest of materials and methods are the same as above.

番茄牛肉炒麵 · *Tomato and Beef Fried Noodle*

熟陽春麵 ----------- 8 8 0公克	菠菜 ----------------- 2 0 0公克
牛肉、番茄------ 各2 4 0公克	洋蔥 ----------------- 1 2 0公克

1
- 水、油 ----------- 各2大匙
- 太白粉、白醋、酒 --------
  ----------------- 各2小匙
- 糖 ------------------ 1小匙
- 鹽 ------------------ ½小匙
- 胡椒粉 -------------- ¼小匙

2
- 高湯 ------------------- 1杯
- 醬油、番茄醬 --各2大匙
- 糖、麻油 -------- 各1小匙
- 鹽 ------------------- ½小匙
- 胡椒粉、味精 --- 各¼小匙

1 牛肉切1×4×0．2公分絲狀，入 **1** 料拌醃，番茄去皮、去籽，切厚片，菠菜洗淨切段，洋蔥切0．5公分寬絲狀。

2 鍋熱入油3大匙燒熱，入洋蔥、番茄炒香，續入牛肉拌炒均勻，再入菠菜、麵條及 **2** 料拌炒均勻即可。

■ 番茄牛肉刀削炒麵：將熟陽春麵改為熟刀削麵，其餘材料及做法同番茄牛肉炒麵。

880g.(2lb.) --- boiled plain noodle	200g.(7oz.) -------- spinach
240g.(8²/₅oz.)each -- beef, tomato	120g.(4¼oz.) -------- onion

1
- •2T.each water, oil
- •2t.each corn starch, white vinegar, cooking wine
- •1t.sugar
- •½t.salt
- •¼t.pepper

2
- •1C.stock
- •2T.each soy sauce, tomato catchup
- •1t.each sugar, sesame oil
- •½t.salt
- •¼t.pepper

1 Shred beef into 1 x 4 x 0.2 cm long shreds, marinate in **1**. Skin tomato, discard seeds, and cut into thick slices. Wash spinach clean and cut into serving sections. Cut onion into 0.5 cm wide shreds.

2 Heat the wok, add 3T. oil and heat to hot; stir fry onion and tomato until fragrant. Stir in beef to fry and mix well; add in spinach, noodle and **2**. Mix evenly and serve.

■ Tomato and Beef Fried Shaved Noodle : Replace boiled plain noodle with boiled shaved noodle. The rest of materials and methods are the same as above.

四人份　**serve 4**

木須肉炒麵 · *Mu-Shu Pork Noodle*

熟陽春麵 ----------- 880公克	880g.(2lb.) ---boiled plain noodle
肉絲 ----------------- 200公克	200g.(7oz.)shredded pork
菠菜 ----------------- 160公克	160g.(5³/₅oz.) -----spinach
濕木耳 -------------- 120公克	120g.(4¼oz.) ------soaked black wood ear
熟筍、胡蘿蔔 ------ 各80公克	80g.(2⁴/₅oz.)each -canned bamboo shoot, carrot
薑 -------------------- 15公克	15g.(½oz.) ----------ginger
蔥段 ------------------- 20段	20 sections --green onion
蛋 --------------------- 4個	4 -----------------------eggs

1
油 ------------------- 2大匙	•2T.oil
醬油、酒 --------- 各1小匙	•1t.each soy sauce, cooking wine
糖 ------------------- ½小匙	•½t.sugar
鹽 ------------------- ¼小匙	•¼t.salt
胡椒粉 -------------- ⅛小匙	•⅛t.pepper

2
高湯 ----------------- ½杯	•½C.stock
醬油 ----------------- 2大匙	•2T.soy sauce
酒 ------------------- 2小匙	•2t.cooking wine
鹽、味精、麻油 各½小匙	•½t.each salt, sesame oil

1 肉絲入 **1** 料拌醃，木耳、熟筍、胡蘿蔔均切0.3×0.2× 4公分絲狀，菠菜洗淨切3～4公分長段，薑切片，蛋打散備用。

2 鍋熱入油2大匙燒熱，入蛋液炒熟盛起。

3 另鍋熱入油3大匙燒熱，入蔥、薑爆香後，依次入胡蘿蔔、肉絲、木耳、筍絲、菠菜後，再入麵條、蛋及 **2** 料炒拌均勻即可。

■ 木須肉刀切麵、木須肉刀削麵：將熟陽春麵改為熟刀切麵或熟刀削麵，其餘材料及做法同木須肉炒麵。

1 Marinate shredded pork in **1**. Shred wood ear, bamboo, and carrot into 0.3 x 0.2 x 4 cm long shreds. Wash spinach clean and cut into 3 ~ 4 cm long sections. Slice ginger. Beat eggs.

2 Heat the wok, add 2T. oil and heat to hot. Stir fry egg, remove.

3 In a clean wok, add 3T. oil and heat to hot; stir fry green onion and ginger until fragrant. Add in by the order of carrot, pork, wood ear, bamboo, and spinach; mix evenly. Then stir in noodle, egg, and **2**; mix well and heat thoroughly. Serve.

■ Mu-Shu Pork Handmade Noodle and Mu-Shu Pork Shaved Noodle : Replace boiled plain noodle with boiled handmade noodle or boiled shaved noodle. The rest of materials and methods are the same as above.

豬肉筍片炒麵 · *Pork and Bamboo Shoot Fried Noodle*

熟陽春麵 ----------- 8 8 0公克		
豬肉 ---------------- 2 0 0公克		
熟筍 ---------------- 1 6 0公克		
洋蔥、高麗菜 -- 各1 4 0公克		
熟洋菇 -------------- 8 0公克		
胡蘿蔔 -------------- 6 0公克		
蒜頭 ---------------- 1 0公克		

❶
- 油 ------------------ 2 大匙
- 醬油、酒 -------- 各1 大匙
- 糖 ------------------ 1 小匙
- 胡椒粉 ------------- ¼小匙

❷
- 高湯 ---------------- 1 杯
- 醬油 --------------- 2 ⅔大匙
- 酒 ------------------ 1 大匙
- 麻油 --------------- 1 小匙
- 鹽、味精 --------- 各¼小匙

1 豬肉切1 · 5×4×0 · 2公分片狀，入 ❶ 料拌醃，熟筍、胡蘿蔔切1×3 · 5×0 · 2公分條狀，洋蔥、高麗菜切粗絲，洋菇切0 · 3公分片狀，蒜切小片。
2 鍋熱入油3 大匙燒熱，入蒜片、洋蔥爆香，續入豬肉、胡蘿蔔、高麗菜、熟筍、洋菇炒熟，再入 ❷ 料及麵條炒拌均勻即可。
■ 豬肉筍片麵之熟陽春麵可以熟刀切麵取代。

880g.(2lb.) --- boiled plain noodle
200g.(7oz.) ----------- pork
160g.(5³/₅oz.) ------ canned bamboo shoot
140g.(5oz.)each --- onion, cabbage
80g.(2⁴/₅oz.) ------- canned mushroom
60g.(2¹/₉oz.) -------- carrot
10g.(¹/₃oz.) ----------- garlic

❶
- 2T.oil
- 1T.each soy sauce, cooking wine
- 1t.sugar
- ¼t.pepper

❷
- 1C.stock
- 2²/₃T.soy sauce
- 1T.cooking wine
- 1t.sesame oil
- ¼t.salt

1 Cut pork into 1.5 x 4 x 0.2 thin slices and marinate in **❶**. Cut bamboo and carrot into 1 x 3.5 x 0.2 cm strips. Shred onion and cabbage coarsely. Cut mushroom in 0.3 thin slices. Slice garlic small.
2 Heat the wok, add 3T. oil and heat to hot. Stir fry garlic slices and onion until fragrant. Add in pork, carrot, cabbage, bamboo, and mushroom to fry until cooked. Mix in **❷** and noodle well and heat thoroughly. Serve.
■ Boiled plain noodle can be replaced by boiled handmade noodle.

咖哩雞炒麵・*Curry Chicken Fried Noodle*

熟陽春麵 ------------ 880公克	
雞胸肉 -------------- 240公克	
高麗菜 -------------- 200公克	
熟筍、洋蔥 ------ 各120公克	
青椒 ------------------- 80公克	
香菇 ------------------- 10公克	
咖哩粉 --------------------- 2大匙	
鹽 ----------------------- ½小匙	

❶
- 高湯 ------------------- ½杯
- 醬油 -------------- 1⅓大匙
- 酒 ------------------ 1 大匙
- 麻油 ---------------- 1 小匙
- 鹽 -------------------- ⅔小匙
- 味精、胡椒粉 --- 各½小匙

1. 雞胸肉洗淨，加鹽拌醃5分鐘後，入鍋大火蒸熟，取出待涼拆絲備用。
2. 香菇泡軟去蒂，與其他材料洗淨後皆切成絲，鍋熱入油3大匙燒熱，入香菇及洋蔥爆香，續入高麗菜、熟筍、青椒炒熟，盛起備用。
3. 另鍋熱入油1大匙燒熱，入咖哩粉炒香，再依次入麵條、**2** 項之材料、雞絲及 **❶** 料炒拌均勻即可。

880g.(2lb.) --- boiled plain noodle
240g.(8²⁄₅oz.) ----- chicken breast
200g.(7oz.) ------ cabbage
120g.(4¼oz.)each canned bamboo shoot, onion
80g.(2⅘oz.) green pepper
10g.(⅓oz.) ----- dried black mushroom
2T. ---------- curry powder
½t. ----------------------- salt

❶
- ½C.stock
- 1⅓T.soy sauce
- 1T.cooking wine
- 1t.sesame oil
- ²⁄₃t.salt
- ½t.pepper

1. Wash chicken breast clean and marinate with salt for 5 minutes, steam over high heat until cooked. When cooled, shred by hand.
2. Soften mushroom in warm water, discard stem; shred as all the other materials. Heat the wok, add 3T. oil and heat to hot; stir fry mushroom and onion until fragrant. Add in cabbage, bamboo, and green pepper to fry until cooked; remove.
3. In a clean wok, add 1T. oil and heat to hot; stir fry curry powder until fragrant. Add in by the order of noodle, materials of **2** , chicken, and **❶**; mix well and heat thoroughly. Serve.

雞火炒麵 • *Chicken and Ham Fried Noodle*

兩面黃 ------------- 680公克		洋火腿 ------------- 130公克		
雞胸肉、大白菜 各240公克		豌豆莢 ------------- 80公克		

1
```
蛋白 ----------------- 1個
油 ------------------- 2大匙
太白粉 -------------- 1⅓大匙
酒 ------------------- 2小匙
鹽 ------------------- ½小匙
味精、胡椒粉 --- 各¼小匙
```

2
```
高湯 ----------------- 3杯
醬油 --------------- 1⅓大匙
酒 ------------------- 2小匙
鹽 ------------------- ⅔小匙
味精 ----------------- ½小匙
```

3
```
水 ------------------- 3大匙
大白粉 ----------- 1⅓大匙
```

1 雞胸肉切如豌豆莢大小之片狀，入 **1** 料拌醃，豌豆莢去老纖維，大白菜洗淨與火腿均切如豌豆莢之片狀。
2 鍋熱入油４杯燒至五分熱（１２０℃），將雞肉入鍋過油至變色，撈起瀝油，再入大白菜及豌豆莢入鍋過油，隨即撈起瀝油。
3 鍋內留油２大匙燒熱，入火腿炒香，續入 **2** 料、雞肉、大白菜、豌豆莢煮開，再以 **3** 料芶芡，淋於兩面黃上即可。
■ 雞火伊麵：將兩面黃改為伊麵，其餘材料及做法同雞火炒麵。

680g.(1½lb.) ------- noodle pancake
240g.(8²/₅oz.)each --------- Chinese cabbage, chicken breast
130g.(4³/₅oz.) ------ virginia ham
80g.(2⁴/₅oz.) ---- snow pea pod

1
```
•1 egg white
•2T.oil
•1⅓T.corn starch
•2t.cooking wine
•½t.salt
•¼t.pepper
```

2
```
•3C.stock
•1⅓T.soy sauce
•2t.cooking wine
•⅔t.salt
```

3
```
•3T.water
•1⅓T.corn starch
```

1 Cut chicken breast into same size slices as snow pea pod, marinate in **1**. Discard tough fibers of snow pea pod. Wash Chinese cabbage clean, cut it and ham into same size slices as snow pea pod.
2 Heat the wok, add 4C. oil and heat to 120°C(248°F). Soak chicken in oil until color turns pale, lift out and drain. Then soak cabbage and snow pea pod in oil , remove immediately.
3 Keep 2T. oil in the wok, stir fry ham until fragrant; add in **2**, chicken, cabbage, and snow pea pod, bring to boil. Thicken with **3**, pour over noodle pancake and serve.
■ Chicken and Ham E-Fu Noodle : Replace noodle pancake with e-fu noodle. The rest of materials and methods are the same as above.

羅漢齋炒麵 · *Vegetarian's Fried Noodle*

兩面黃 -------------- ６８０公克
麵腸、青江菜 ---各１２０公克
胡蘿蔔、濕木耳、熟筍 ---------
------------------------各６０公克
炸豆皮 ----------------- ３０公克
麵筋泡 ----------------- ２０公克
香菇 -------------------- １６公克

<table>
<tr><td rowspan="6">■</td><td>高湯 ------------------ ２½杯</td></tr>
<tr><td>醬油 ----------------- ２大匙</td></tr>
<tr><td>太白粉 -------------- １大匙</td></tr>
<tr><td>蠔油 ----------------- ２小匙</td></tr>
<tr><td>糖 -------------------- １小匙</td></tr>
<tr><td>味精、鹽 --------- 各½小匙</td></tr>
</table>

1 麵腸切０・３公分片狀，香菇泡軟去蒂切１公分條狀，豆皮切
　　１・５×４公分片狀，與麵筋泡均泡水去油脂，熟筍、胡蘿蔔、
　　濕木耳洗淨，切１×４公分條狀，青江菜洗淨一切成４。
2 鍋熱入油３大匙燒熱，入香菇爆香，續入其餘材料炒軟，再入 ■
　　料煮開，淋於兩面黃上即可。

680g.(1½lb.) ------- noodle pancake
120g.(4¼oz.)each - wheat gluten, bok choy
60g.(2⅑oz.)each --- carrot, soaked black wood ear, canned bamboo shoot
30g.(1oz.) ------ fried bean curd skin
20g.(⅔oz.) --- fried gluten puff
16g.(³/₅oz.) ---- dried black mushroom

- 2½C.stock
- 2T.soy sauce
- 1T.corn starch
- 2t.oyster sauce
- 1t.sugar
- ½t.salt

1 Cut wheat gluten into 0.3 cm slices. Soften mushroom in warm water, discard stems. Cut bean curd skin into 1.5 x 4 cm slices; and soak with fried gluten puff in water to rid of grease. Wash clean bamboo, carrot, and wood ear; cut all into 1 x 4 cm strips. Wash bok choy clean and cut into quarters.
2 Heat the wok, add 3T. oil and heat to hot. Stir fry mushroom until fragrant, add in the rest of materials to stir fry until all softened. Add in ■ and bring to boil. Pour over noodle pancake and serve.

銀芽三絲麵 • *Three Shreds and Bean Sprout Noodle*

兩面黃 -------------- 680公克	
銀芽 ----------------- 225公克	
肉絲 ----------------- 200公克	
韭黃 ----------------- 160公克	
香菇 -------------------- 16公克	

1　油 -------------------- 2大匙
　　水、醬油 -------- 各1大匙
　　太白粉 ------------- 1小匙

2　高湯 -------------------- 2杯
　　醬油 -------------- 1⅓大匙
　　糖、太白粉 ----- 各1小匙
　　鹽、味精 --------- 各½小匙

1 肉絲入 **1** 料拌醃，韭黃洗淨切3公分段，香菇泡軟去蒂切0‧2公分絲狀。

2 鍋熱入油3大匙燒熱，入香菇絲爆香，續入肉絲、銀芽、韭黃炒勻，再加 **2** 料煮開，淋於兩面黃上即可。

680g.(1½lb.) ------- noodle pancake
225g.(8oz.) -- bean sprout
200g.(7oz.)shredded pork
160g.(5⅗oz.) yellow chive
16g.(⅗oz.) ---- dried black mushroom

1
• 2T.oil
• 1T.each water, soy sauce
• 1t.corn starch

2
• 2C.stock
• 1⅓T.soy sauce
• 1t.each sugar, corn starch
• ½t.salt

1 Marinate pork in **1** . Wash clean chive and cut into 3 cm sections. Soften mushroom in warm water, discard stems, and shred to 0.2 cm shreds.

2 Heat the wok, add 3T. oil and heat to hot; stir fry mushroom until fragrant. Stir in pork, bean sprout, and chive; mix well. Add in **2** and bring to boil. Pour over noodle pancake and serve.

金華炒麵 · *Chin Hua Style Fried Noodle*

熟陽春麵 ----------- 8 8 0公克　　高湯 ----------------------- 2杯
蔥段 ----------------------- 2 0段

1[肉絲 ----------- 1 5 0公克
　　中式火腿絲 -- 1 0 0公克

2[大白菜絲 ----- 2 4 0公克
　　熟筍絲 --------- 1 2 0公克
　　胡蘿蔔絲 -------- 8 0公克

3[醬油 ----------------- 2 大匙
　　糖 ------------------- 1 大匙
　　酒、太白粉 ----- 各 2 小匙
　　麻油 ----------------- 1 小匙
　　味精、胡椒粉 --- 各½小匙

1 鍋熱入油 3 大匙燒熱，蔥段爆香，入 **1** 料及高湯煮開，改小火
燜煮 1 0 分鐘後入 **2** 料煮熟，再入 **3** 料及麵條炒拌均勻即可。

880g.(2lb.) --- boiled plain noodle
20 sections -- green onion
2C. ---------------------- stock

1[•150g.(5⅓oz.) shredded pork
　　•100g.(3½oz.) shredded Chinese ham

2[•240g.(8²/₅oz.) shredded Chinese cabbage
　　•120g.(4¼oz.) shredded canned bamboo shoot
　　•80g.(2⅘oz.) shredded carrot

3[•2T.soy sauce
　　•1T.sugar
　　•2t.each cooking wine, corn starch
　　•1t.sesame oil
　　•½t.pepper

四人份　**serve 4**

1 Heat the wok, add 3T. oil and heat to hot; stir fry green onion until fragrant. Add in **1** and stock, bring to boil; simmer over low heat for 10 minutes. Stir in **2** and cook until all done. Add in **3** and noodle; mix well and heat thoroughly. Serve.

鮑魚銀芽麵 · *Abalone and Bean Sprout Fried Noodle*

熟陽春麵 ----------- 8 8 0公克
紅辣椒 ----------------- 1 0公克

1[銀芽 ----------- 2 2 5公克
　　韭黃 ----------- 1 6 0公克
　　鮑魚 ----------- 1 2 0公克

2[鮑魚湯 ------------------ ½杯
　　酒、醬油 ------ 各 1 ⅓大匙
　　麻油、鹽 --------- 各⅔小匙
　　味精、胡椒粉 --- 各¼小匙

1 鮑魚切細絲，紅辣椒去籽亦切細絲，韭黃洗淨切 3～4 公分段。
2 鍋熱入油 3 大匙燒熱，入 **1** 料炒勻，續入 **2** 料、麵條拌炒均勻，
再入紅辣椒拌勻即可。
■ 鮑魚銀芽麵之熟陽春麵可以熟油麵取代。

880g.(2lb.) --- boiled plain noodle
10g.(⅓oz.) ----- red pepper

1[•225g.(8oz.) bean sprout
　　•160g.(5³/₅oz.) yellow chive
　　•120g.(4¼oz.) canned abalone

2[•½C.abalone juice
　　•1⅓T.each cooking wine, soy sauce
　　•⅔t.each sesame oil, salt
　　•¼t.pepper

1 Shred abalone thin. Discard seeds in red pepper and shred thin. Wash chive clean and cut into 3 ~ 4 cm long sections.
2 Heat the wok, add 3T. oil and heat to hot; stir in **1** to fry evenly. Add in **2** and noodle, stir fry and mix well. Mix in red pepper and serve.
■ Boiled plain noodle can be replaced by boiled yellow noodle.

　四人份　**serve 4**

福建炒麵 • *Fu Kien Style Fried Noodle*

熟陽春麵 ---------- 880公克　　洋蔥絲、熟筍絲 各120公克
肉絲、大白菜絲 各240公克　　熟青豆仁 -------------- 30公克

1［蝦米 ------------- 20公克
　　香菇 ------------- 12公克

2［油 ------------------- 2 大匙
　　醬油、酒 -------- 各1 大匙

3［高湯 ------------------- ½杯
　　醬油 ---------------- 2 大匙
　　鹽、味精 -------- 各½小匙
　　胡椒粉 --------------- ¼小匙

1 肉絲入 **2** 料拌醃，香菇泡軟去蒂切絲，蝦米泡軟剁碎。
2 鍋熱入油3 大匙燒熱，入洋蔥及 **1** 料炒香，續入肉絲、大白菜、
　　熟筍炒熟，再入青豆仁、**3** 料及麵條炒拌均勻即可。

880g.(2lb.) ---boiled plain noodle
240g.(8²/₅oz.)each --------- shredded pork, shredded Chinese cabbage
120g.(4¹/₄oz.)each --------- shredded onion, shredded canned bamboo shoot
30g.(1oz.) -canned green peas

1［•20g.(²/₃oz.) dried baby shrimp
　　•12g.(²/₅oz.) dried black mushroom

2［•2T.oil
　　•1T.each soy sauce, cooking wine

3［•½C.stock
　　•2T.soy sauce
　　•½t.salt
　　•¼t.pepper

1 Marinate pork in **2**. Soften mushroom in warm water, discard stems and shred. Soften dried shrimp in water and chop fine.
2 Heat the wok, add 3T. oil and heat to hot; stir fry onion and **1** until fragrant. Add in pork, cabbage, and bamboo; stir fry until all cooked. Mix in green peas, **3**, and noodle well; heat thoroughly. Serve.

四人份　　**serve 4**

廣州炒麵 • *Guang Zhou Style Fried Noodle*

兩面黃 -------------- 680公克

1［叉燒肉、瘦肉、魚肉淨重
　　、花枝片、蝦仁、豌豆莢
　　-------------- 各80公克

2［高湯 ------------------- 2½杯
　　醬油 ---------------- 2 大匙
　　太白粉 -------------- 1 大匙
　　糖、麻油 -------- 各1 小匙
　　味精、鹽 -------- 各¼小匙

1 蝦仁去腸泥洗淨，豌豆莢去老纖維洗淨，其餘 **1** 料均切薄片。
2 鍋熱入油4 大匙燒熱，入 **1** 料炒勻，再入 **2** 料煮開，盛起淋於
　　兩面黃上即可。

680g.(1½lb.) ------ noodle pancake

1［•80g.(2⁴/₅oz.)each Bar-B-Q pork, lean pork, fish fillet (net weight), squid, shelled shrimp, snow pea pod

2［•2½C.stock
　　•2T.soy sauce
　　•1T.corn starch
　　•1t.each sugar, sesame oil
　　•¼t.salt

1 Devein shrimp and rinse clean. Discard tough fibers on snow pea pod. Cut all the rest of materials in **1** into thin slices.
2 Heat the wok, add 4T. oil and heat to hot; stir fry **1** evenly and well. Add in **2** and bring to boil. Pour over noodle pancake and serve.

四人份　　**serve 4**

揚州炒麵 · *Yang Zhou Style Fried Noodle*

兩面黃 -------------- ６８０公克

1
- 雞胸肉、海參、花枝 ----- ----------各６０公克
- 蝦仁 ------------- ５０公克
- 叉燒肉、中式火腿 -------- ----------各４０公克
- 雞心、雞肝、雞胗 各2付

3
- 高湯 -------------------- ２杯
- 醬油 -------------------- ２大匙
- 太白粉 ----------- １⅓大匙
- 糖 ---------------------- １小匙
- 鹽、胡椒粉、味精 -------- --------------------各¼小匙

2
- 熟草菇 ----------- ８０公克
- 熟筍、熟毛豆各６０公克

1 將 **1** 料及筍切約１．５公分之方形小片，草菇切０．３公分薄片。

2 鍋熱入油３大匙燒熱，入 **1** 料炒勻，續入 **2** 料及 **3** 料煮開，再淋於兩面黃上即可。

680g.(1½lb.) ------- noodle pancake

1
- •60g.(2¹/₉oz.)each chicken breast, squid, sea cucumber
- •50g.(1³/₄oz.) shelled shrimp
- •40g.(1²/₅oz.)each Bar-B-Q pork, Chinese ham
- •2 sets each chicken heart, chicken liver, chicken gizzard

2
- •80g.(2⁴/₅oz.) canned straw mushroom
- •60g.(2¹/₉oz.)each canned bamboo shoot, boiled fresh soy bean

3
- •2C.stock
- •2T.soy sauce
- •1⅓T.corn starch
- •1t.sugar
- •¼t.each salt, pepper

1 Cut all materials of **1** and bamboo into 1.5 cm square small slices. Slice straw mushroom into 0.3 cm slices.

2 Heat the wok, add 3T. oil and heat to hot. Stir fry all materials well and mix evenly. Add in **2** and **3**, bring to boil. Pour over noodle pancake and serve.

蝦茸窩麵 • *Minced Shrimp Potagé Noodle*

熟陽春麵 ----------- 880公克	熟筍片、豌豆莢 --- 各50公克
蝦仁 ----------------- 260公克	高湯 ------------------------- 8杯
熟洋菇片 ----------- 100公克	蔥段 ------------------------- 4段

1
┌ 蛋白 ----------------------1個
│ 蔥末 ---------------- 1¼大匙
│ 薑末 ------------------ ½大匙
│ 酒、麻油 -------- 各1小匙
│ 鹽 ------------------------ ½小匙
│ 味精、糖 ---------各¼小匙
└ 胡椒粉 ----------------- ⅛小匙

2
┌ 鹽、麻油 -------- 各1小匙
│ 味精 ------------------- ¼小匙
└ 胡椒粉 ---------------- ⅛小匙

3
┌ 水 ------------------------ 3大匙
└ 太白粉 ------------- 2大匙

1 蝦仁去腸泥洗淨剁碎，入 **1** 料拌打成蝦茸。
2 鍋熱入油3大匙燒熱，入蔥段爆香，續入洋菇、筍及蝦茸炒散
後，再入高湯及 **2** 料煮開，以 **3** 料芶芡，再入麵條續煮3分鐘，
最後再入豌豆莢煮熟即可。

880g.(2lb.) --- boiled plain
noodle
260g.(9oz.)shelled shrimp
100g.(3½oz.) ------ canned
mushroom slices
50g.(1¾oz.)each - canned
bamboo shoot slices,
snow pea pod
8C. --------------------- stock
4 sections ---- green onion

1
• 1 egg white
• 1¼T.minced green
onion
• ½T.minced ginger
• 1t.each cooking wine,
sesame oil
• ½t.salt
• ¼t.sugar
• ⅛t.pepper

2
• 1t.each salt, sesame
oil
• ⅛t.pepper

3
• 3T.water
• 2T.corn starch

1 Devein shrimp, rinse clean, and chop fine. Marinate in
1 and beat it to form shrimp paste.
2 Heat the wok, add 3T. oil and heat to hot. Stir fry
green onion sections until fragrant. Add in
mushroom, bamboo, and shrimp paste, stir fry and
loosen up shrimp paste. Pour in stock and **2**, bring to
boil; thicken with **3**. Add in noodle to cook for 3
minutes. Stir in snow pea pod, boil until cooked.
Serve.

.Taiwanese Potagé Noodle

四人份 **serve 4**

台式燴麵 • *Taiwanese Potagé Noodle*

熟陽春麵 ----------- 880公克	
大白菜 ------------- 200公克	
梅花絞肉 ----------- 150公克	
花枝淨重 ----------- 80公克	
熟筍 --------------- 50公克	
豌豆莢、叉燒肉 --- 各40公克	
香菇 --------------- 8公克	
高湯 --------------- 8杯	
劍蝦 --------------- 8隻	
蛋 ----------------- 2個	
蔥末 --------------- 2½大匙	

1
- 蛋白 --------------- ½個
- 太白粉 ------------- 1大匙
- 蔥末 --------------- ½大匙
- 鹽、味精 -------- 各¼小匙
- 胡椒粉 ------------- ⅛小匙

3
- 水 ----------------- 3大匙
- 太白粉 ------------- 2大匙

2
- 鹽 ----------------- 1½小匙
- 麻油、酒 -------- 各1小匙
- 味精、糖 -------- 各¼小匙
- 胡椒粉 ------------- ⅛小匙

1 大白菜洗淨切3×4公分片狀，絞肉入 **1** 料拌醃後，捏成直徑3公分的肉丸，豌豆莢去老纖維，叉燒肉、筍切2.5×4公分薄片，香菇泡軟去蒂切絲，劍蝦去腸泥剪鬚，花枝切2×4公分長條花刀，蛋煮熟去殼切半及。

2 鍋熱入油3大匙燒熱，入蔥末及香菇爆香，續入花枝、筍拌炒，再入白菜炒軟後，入高湯煮開，續入 **2** 料及肉丸煮熟後，再入豌豆莢、劍蝦煮開，以 **3** 料芶芡，再入麵條續煮3分鐘，盛起再鋪上白煮蛋及叉燒肉即可。

880g.(2lb.) --------------------------------- boiled plain noodle	
200g.(7oz.) ---------------------------------- Chinese cabbage	
150g.(5⅓oz.) ------------------------- minced pork shoulder	
80g.(2⅘oz.) --------------------------- squid (net weight)	
50g.(1¾oz.) ------------------------ canned bamboo shoot	
40g.(1⅖oz.) each ---------- snow pea pod, Bar-B-Q pork	
8g.(¼oz.) ----------------------------- dried black mushroom	
8C. --- stock	
8 -- shrimp	
2 --- eggs	
2½T. -------------------------------- minced green onion	

1
- ½ egg white
- 1T. corn starch
- ½T. minced green onion
- ¼t. salt
- ⅛t. pepper

2
- 1½t. salt
- 1t. each sesame oil, cooking wine
- ¼t. sugar
- ⅛t. pepper

3
- 3T. water
- 2T. corn starch

1 Wash cabbage clean and cut into 3 x 4 cm slices. Marinate pork in **1** for a while, squeeze by hand into 3 cm diameter meat balls. Discard tough fibers of pea pod. Cut Bar-B-Q pork and bamboo into 2.5 x 4 cm thin slices. Soften black mushroom in warm water, discard stem, and shred. Devein shrimp, trim off feelers. Cut squid into 2 x 4 cm long pieces. Hard boil eggs and cut into halves.

2 Heat the wok, add 3T. oil and heat to hot. Stir fry minced green onion and mushroom until fragrant. Add in squid and bamboo to fry, then add in cabbage to fry until softened. Pour in stock and bring to boil, add in **2** and meat balls, boil until cooked. Add in pea pod and shrimp, bring to boil again. Thicken with **3**, add in noodle and continue cooking for 3 minutes. Remove into individual bowls, arrange egg halves and Bar-B-Q pork on top, and serve.

川味魚塊麵

.*Szechwan Fish Potagé Noodle*

四人份　**serve　4**

川味魚塊麵 · *Szechwan Fish Potagé Noodle*

熟陽春麵	880公克
鱈魚	175公克
青椒	130公克
西洋芹	100公克
新鮮香菇	70公克
紅辣椒	55公克
高湯	8杯
蔥末	5大匙
蒜末	1½大匙
薑末	1大匙

1
- 酒 ------------ ½小匙
- 鹽 ------------ ¼小匙
- 胡椒粉、味精 --- 各⅛小匙

2
- 低筋麵粉 ------------ ⅗杯
- 水 ------------ ¼杯
- 蛋 ------------ 1個
- 太白粉 ------------ 1½大匙
- 油 ------------ 1小匙
- 泡打粉 ------------ ¼小匙

3
- 豆瓣醬 ------------ 2大匙
- 醬油、麻油 ----- 各1大匙
- 鹽、酒、糖 ----- 各1小匙
- 味精 ------------ ¼小匙
- 胡椒粉 ------------ ⅛小匙

4
- 水 ------------ 4大匙
- 太白粉 ------------ 2大匙

1 鱈魚切1×5公分條狀，以 **1** 料醃約20分鐘，**2** 料調勻成麵糊備用。

2 鍋熱入油4杯燒至八分熱（180℃），魚肉裹上麵糊入油鍋炸至金黃色撈起。

3 青椒、紅辣椒均去籽，西洋芹去老纖維均切0．5×0．5公分丁狀，香菇去蒂切丁。

4 鍋熱入油3大匙燒熱，入蒜末、薑末炒香，續入青椒、紅辣椒、香菇、西洋芹拌炒，以 **3** 料調味，再入高湯煮開，並以 **4** 料芶芡即為麵湯。

5 麵條置於碗中，上置魚塊淋上麵湯並灑上蔥末即可。

880g.(2lb.)	boiled plain noodle
175g.(6¹/₇oz.)	halibut fillet
130g.(4³/₅oz.)	green pepper
100g.(3½oz.)	celery
70g.(2½oz.)	fresh black mushroom
55g.(2oz.)	red pepper
8C.	stock
5T.	minced green onion
1½T.	minced garlic
1T.	minced ginger

1
- ½t.cooking wine
- ¼t.salt
- ⅛t.pepper

2
- ⅗C.low gluten flour
- ¼C.water
- 1 egg
- 1½T.corn starch
- 1t.oil
- ¼t.baking powder

3
- 2T.soy bean paste
- 1T.each soy sauce, sesame oil
- 1t.each salt, cooking wine, sugar
- ⅛t.pepper

4
- 4T.water
- 2T.corn starch

1 Cut halibut fillet into 1 x 5 cm long strips, marinate with **1** for 20 minutes. Mix well **2** to be a flour batter.

2 Heat the wok, add 4C. oil and heat to 180℃ (356° F). Coat fish with flour batter and deep fry until golden.

3 Discard seeds in green and red pepper, tough fibers of celery; cut all three into 0.5 x 0.5 cm dices. Discard stem of mushroom and dice.

4 Heat the wok, add 3T. oil and heat to hot. Stir fry minced garlic and minced ginger until fragrant, add in green pepper, red pepper, mushroom, and celery to fry. Season with **3**, pour in stock and bring to boil. Thicken with **4** to be the potagé .

5 Place noodle in individual bowls, arrange fish fillet on top, pour potagé over, and sprinkle on minced green onion. Serve.

虱目魚羹麵 · *Milk Fish Potagé Noodle*

熟陽春麵 ----------- ８８０公克	
虱目魚1尾 ------ 約６００公克	
魚漿 ----------------- １００公克	
絞肥肉 ----------------- ５０公克	
薑絲、蔥絲 --------- 各４０公克	
高湯 ----------------------- 8 杯	
芹菜末 -------------------- 3 大匙	

1 ┌ 太白粉、酒、麻油 --------
　　└ ---------------------- 各 1 小匙
　　　鹽 ------------------- ½小匙
　　　味精 ---------------- ¼小匙

2 ┌ 鹽、酒、麻油 -- 各 1 小匙
　　└ 味精 ---------------- ½小匙

3 ┌ 水 -------------------- 3 大匙
　　└ 太白粉 ----------- 2½大匙

1 虱目魚洗淨，對剖去大骨取淨肉，用湯匙刮下魚肉並去魚刺後，將魚肉與魚漿、絞肥肉及 **1** 料拌勻並甩打數下，即為虱目魚漿。

2 一鍋水燒至７０℃，將虱目魚漿捏成長約４公分之橢圓條入鍋煮至浮起即撈出，是為虱目魚羹。

3 另將高湯及 **2** 料煮開，入虱目魚羹及薑、蔥絲煮開，以 **3** 料芶芡即為虱目魚羹湯。

4 麵條置於碗中，灑上芹菜末再淋上虱目魚羹湯即可。

■ 虱目魚羹之熟陽春麵可以熟油麵取代。

880g.(2lb.) ---boiled plain noodle
600g.(1⅓lb.) --one whole milk fish
100g.(3½oz.) ---fish paste
50g.(1¾oz.) ------- minced. pork fat
40g.(1⅖oz.)each ---------- shredded ginger,shredded green onion
8C. --------------------stock
3T. ---------minced celery

1 ┌ •1t.each corn starch, cooking wine,sesame oil
　　└ •½t.salt

2 ┌ •1t.each salt, cooking wine, sesame oil

3 ┌ •3T.water
　　└ •2½T.corn starch

1 Wash milk fish clean, cut into halves lengthwise, remove the center bone. With a spoon, scrape off fish meat and remove all small bones. Mix well fish meat, fish paste, minced pork fat, and **1**; beat and throw a few times. This is the milk fish paste.

2 Heat a pot of water to 70°C (158°F), squeeze milk fish paste into oblong strips and drop into the hot water. Lift out when floating over the water.

3 Bring stock and **2** to boil, add in milk fish strips, ginger, and green onion; bring to boil again. Thicken with **3** to be the potagé.

4 Place noodle in individual bowls, sprinkle on minced celery. Pour over potagé and serve.

■ Boiled plain noodle can be replaced by boiled yellow noodle.

蟹肉羹麵 · *Crab Meat Potagé Noodle*

熟陽春麵 ---------- 880公克	
螃蟹2隻 ---------- 800公克	
熟洋菇 ------------- 50公克	
高湯 -------------------- 8杯	
蔥段 ----------------- 25段	
薑片 ------------------- 2片	

❶
- 水 -------------------- ½杯
- 薑片 ----------------- 2片
- 酒 ------------------- 2小匙

❷
- 醬油 ----------------- 2大匙
- 烏醋 ----------------- 1大匙
- 糖 ------------------- 2小匙
- 麻油、酒 ------- 各1小匙
- 鹽 -------------------- ¼小匙
- 胡椒粉 -------------- ⅛小匙

❸
- 水 ------------------- 3大匙
- 太白粉 ------------- 2大匙

880g.(2lb.) ---boiled plain noodle
800g.(1¾lb.) ------2 crabs
50g.(1¾oz.) -------canned mushroom
8C. --------------------stock
25 sections --green onion
2 slices --------------ginger

❶
- ½C.water
- 2 slices ginger
- 2t.cooking wine

❷
- 2T.soy sauce
- 1T.brown vinegar
- 2t.sugar
- 1t.each sesame oil, cooking wine
- ¼t.salt
- ⅛t.pepper

❸
- 3T.water
- 2T.corn starch

1 蟹揭開殼蓋去除腮及內臟後洗淨，入 **❶** 料蒸25分鐘取出（蒸汁留用），待涼剝殼取肉，洋菇切片備用。

2 鍋熱入豬油4大匙燒熱，入蔥段、薑片炒香，續入蟹肉、洋菇略炒，再入高湯及蒸汁煮開並以 **❷** 料調味後，再入麵條略煮至入味後，以 **❸** 料勾芡即可。

1 Pull off the upper shell of crab, remove the gills and entrails thoroughly. Wash crab clean, pour over **❶**, and steam for 25 minutes, remove (keep juice for later use). When cooled, peel off the shell and remove all crab meat. Slice mushroom.

2 Heat the wok, add 4T. lard and heat to hot. Stir fry green onion sections and ginger slices until fragrant. Add in crab meat and mushroom to stir fry. Pour in stock and juice and bring to boil, season with **❷**. Add in noodle and cook until tasty. Thicken with **❸** and serve.

永滷刀削麵・*Toen-Lu Potagé Shaved Noodle*

熟刀削麵 ----------- ８８０公克
小黃瓜丁 ---------- １５０公克
熟筍丁、鮑魚丁、熟洋菇丁 ---
-------------------------- 各７０公克
里肌肉、雞胸肉 --- 各５０公克
蝦仁、海參 -------- 各４５公克

干貝2顆 ----------- 約１０公克
高湯 ------------------------- 9杯
蛋 --------------------------- 2個
蔥末 --------------------- 2½大匙
薑末 --------------------- ⅓大匙

❶
太白粉 ----------------- 1大匙
麻油 -------------------- ½大匙
鹽、味精、酒 --- 各¼小匙
胡椒粉 ---------------- ⅛小匙

❷
麻油 ----------------- 1大匙
鹽 ------------------ 1¼小匙
酒 ------------------- ½小匙
味精、胡椒粉 --- 各¼小匙

1 里肌肉、雞胸肉、蝦仁、海參均洗淨，切小丁混合均勻，以 **❶** 料醃30分鐘備用。
2 蛋打散，干貝加水蒸軟壓絲，干貝汁留下備用。
3 鍋熱入油３大匙燒熱，入蔥、薑末爆香，續入高湯及干貝蒸汁煮開，再入 **1** 項之材料與干貝蒸汁煮2分鐘後，入筍丁、鮑魚丁、洋菇丁煮開，以 **❷** 料調味，最後入蛋液及小黃瓜丁煮開即為麵湯。
4 麵條置於碗中，淋上麵湯即可。
■ 永滷麵、永滷貓耳朵：將熟刀削麵改為熟陽春麵或熟貓耳朵，其餘材料及做法同永滷刀削麵。

880g.(2lb.) ---------- boiled shaved noodle
150g.(5⅓oz.) - diced baby cucumber
70g.(2½oz.)each ---- diced canned bamboo shoot, diced abalone, diced canned mushroom

50g.(1¾oz.)each ----- pork fillet, chicken breast
45g.(1⅗oz.)each -- shelled shrimp, sea cucumber
10g.(⅓oz.) 2 dried scallop
9C. --------------------- stock
2 ----------------------- eggs
2½T. minced green onion
⅓T. --------- minced ginger

❶
• 1T.corn starch
• ½T.sesame oil
• ¼t.each salt, cooking wine
• ⅛t.pepper

❷
• 1T.sesame oil
• 1¼t.salt
• ½t.cooking wine
• ¼t.pepper

1 Rinse clean pork fillet, chicken breast, shrimp, and sea cucumber; dice all and mix well. Marinate in **❶** for 30 minutes.
2 Beat eggs. Steam dried scallop with some water to soften and shred, keep scallop juice for later use.
3 Heat the wok, add 3T. oil and heat to hot. Stir fry minced green onion and minced ginger until fragrant, add in stock and scallop juice, continue boiling for 2 minutes. Add in bamboo, abalone, and mushroom; bring to boil again. Season with **❷**, stir in beatened eggs and cucumber. Bring to boil once more to be the toen-lu potagé.
4 Place noodle in individual bowls, pour over toen-lu potagé and serve.
■ Toen-Lu Potagé Noodle and Toen-Lu Potagé Cat's Ears : Replace boiled shaved noodle with boiled plain noodle or boiled cat's ears.The rest of materials and methods are the same as above.

酸辣雞丁麵 • *Spicy and Sour Chicken Potagé Noodle*

熟陽春麵 ----------- 880公克	高湯 ------------------------- 8杯	880g.(2lb.) --- boiled plain noodle	240g.(8²/₅oz.) --- bok choy
雞胸肉 -------------- 250公克	蔥末 ------------------------- 5大匙	250g.(8⁴/₅oz.) ----- chicken breast	8C. --------------------- stock
青江菜 -------------- 240公克			5T. -- minced green onion

1
- 蛋白 -------------------- 1個
- 太白粉 ------------------ 1大匙
- 蒜末、紅辣椒末 各²/₃大匙
- 醬油、酒、烏醋、麻油 -- 各½大匙
- 糖、鹽、薑末 --- 各½小匙
- 辣椒粉 ----------------- ¼小匙

2
- 醬油、烏醋 ----- 各3大匙
- 冰糖、麻油 ----- 各1小匙
- 辣椒粉 ---------------- ½小匙
- 鹽、味精 --------- 各¼小匙

1
- •1 egg white
- •1T. corn starch
- •²/₃T. each minced garlic, minced red pepper
- •½T. each soy sauce, cooking wine, brown vinegar, sesame oil
- •½t. each sugar, salt, minced ginger
- •¼t. chili powder

2
- •3T. each soy sauce, brown vinegar
- •1t. each crystal sugar, sesame oil
- •½t. chili powder
- •¼t. salt

1 雞胸肉切1‧5立方公分小丁，以 **1** 料醃30分鐘，青江菜洗淨剝成一片片備用。

2 鍋熱入油3大匙燒熱，入雞丁炒熟後撈起，肉汁留鍋中再加入高湯及 **2** 料煮開，入青江菜煮熟即為麵湯。

3 麵條置於碗中，上置雞丁，灑上蔥末，再淋上麵湯即可。

1 Cut chicken into 1.5 cm square cubes, marinate in **1** for 30 minutes. Peel off bok choy leaf by leaf and wash clean.

2 Heat the wok, add 3T. oil and heat to hot; stir fry chicken until cooked, lift out. Keep the juice in the wok, add in stock and **2**, bring to boil. Add in bok choy to boil until cooked. This is the noodle soup.

3 Place noodle in individual bowls, arrange chicken on top. Sprinkle on minced green onion. Pour over noodle soup and serve.

蝦仁菠菜麵 • *Shrimp Spinach Noodle*

熟菠菜麵 ---------- 880公克		880g.(2lb.) ---------- boiled spinach noodle	
蝦仁 ---------------- 300公克		300g.(10½oz.) ----- shelled shrimp	
熟青豆仁 ---------- 100公克		100g.(3½oz.) ------- boiled green peas	
薑末 ------------------ 2大匙		2T. ---------- minced ginger	
蔥末 --------------- 1¼大匙		1¼T. minced green onion	
蒜末 ------------------ 1大匙		1T. ---------- minced garlic	
白醋 ------------------ 1小匙		1t. ---------- white vinegar	

1
- 蛋白 ----------------- 1個
- 太白粉 ------------- 2大匙
- 油 --------------------- 2小匙
- 鹽 ---------------------¼小匙

1
- •1 egg white
- •2T.corn starch
- •2t.oil
- •¼t.salt

2
- 高湯 ----------------- 1½杯
- 番茄醬 ------------- 5大匙
- 酒 --------------------- 2大匙
- 糖 --------------------- 1大匙
- 豆瓣醬 ------------- 2小匙
- 鹽 ------------------ 1¼小匙

2
- •1½C.stock
- •5T.tomato catchup
- •2T.cooking wine
- •1T.sugar
- •2t.soy bean paste
- •1¼t.salt

3
- 水 ------------------ 1⅓大匙
- 太白粉 ------------- 2小匙

3
- •1⅓T.water
- •2t.corn starch

1 蝦仁去腸泥洗淨，入**1**料拌醃10分鐘後，入油鍋中過油至熟，取出瀝油備用。

2 鍋熱入油2大匙燒熱，入薑末、蒜末爆香，再入蝦仁、青豆仁、蔥末及**2**料煮開，以**3**料芶芡，最後淋上白醋即為拌麵料。

3 麵條置於盤上，淋上拌麵料拌勻即可。

1 Devein shrimp and wash clean, marinate with **1** for 10 minutes; soak in hot oil until cooked, lift out and drain.

2 Heat the wok, add 2T. oil and heat to hot; stir fry ginger and garlic until fragrant. Add in shrimp, green peas, green onion, and **2**, bring to boil; thicken with **3**. Sprinkle on vinegar to be the sauce.

3 Place noodle on a plate, pour sauce over and mix well before serving.

青豆鮪魚拌麵・*Tuna Fish Noodle*

熟陽春麵 ----------- ８８０公克	熟青豆仁 -------------- ６０公克	880g.(2lb.) ---boiled plain noodle	80g.(2⁴/₅oz.)each --celery, carrot
罐頭鮪魚 ----------- ２４０公克	鮮奶油 -------------------- ４大匙		
西洋芹、胡蘿蔔 ---各８０公克	白芝麻 ------------------- １¹/₃大匙		

熟陽春麵 ----------- ８８０公克
罐頭鮪魚 ----------- ２４０公克
西洋芹、胡蘿蔔 ---各８０公克
熟青豆仁 -------------- ６０公克
鮮奶油 -------------------- ４大匙
白芝麻 ------------------- １¹/₃大匙

1
┌ 高湯 ------------------- 1 杯
│ 白葡萄酒 ----------- 6 大匙
┤ 太白粉 -------------- 2 小匙
│ 鹽 -------------------- 1 小匙
└ 胡椒粉 -------------- ¹/₄小匙

1 鮪魚略為壓碎，西洋芹、胡蘿蔔洗淨，切約 1 公分立方小丁，白芝麻炒熟備用。

2 鍋熱入油 3 大匙燒熱，依次入胡蘿蔔、西洋芹炒熟，續入鮪魚、青豆仁、**1**料煮開，再入鮮奶油拌勻，淋於麵條上，再灑上芝麻即可。

880g.(2lb.) ---boiled plain noodle
240g.(8²/₅oz.)------canned tuna fish
4T. ------------fresh cream
80g.(2⁴/₅oz.)each --celery, carrot
60g.(2¹/₉oz.) ---------boiled green peas
1¹/₃T. ---------white sesame

1
┌ •1C.stock
│ •6T.white wine
┤ •2t.corn starch
│ •1t.salt
└ •¹/₄t.pepper

1 Break tuna fish lump loose. Wash celery and carrot clean, cut into 1 cm square slices. Stir fry sesame until done.

2 Heat the wok, add 3T. oil and heat to hot; add in carrot and celery, stir fry until cooked. Add in tuna fish, green peas, and **1**, bring to boil. Mix in cream and pour over noodle. Sprinkle on sesame and serve.

白果辣醬拌麵 · *Spicy Ginkgo Nut Noodle*

熟陽春麵 ---------- 880公克	熟白果 ---------- 100公克
雞胸肉 ----------- 300公克	熟洋菇、熟青豆仁 各50公克
筍 ------------- 120公克	

1
- 酒、油 -------- 各2小匙
- 太白粉 --------- 1小匙
- 鹽 ----------- 1/2小匙
- 胡椒粉 --------- 1/4小匙

3
- 高湯 ---------- 2杯
- 酒 ----------- 2小匙
- 糖 ----------- 1小匙
- 鹽、胡椒粉 ----- 各1/2小匙
- 味精 ---------- 1/4小匙

2
- 甜麵醬 -------- 1 1/3大匙
- 豆瓣醬、辣豆瓣醬 --------
  ----------- 各2小匙

4
- 水 ---------- 1 1/3大匙
- 太白粉 -------- 2小匙

1 雞胸肉切1公分立方小丁，入 **1** 料拌醃，筍、洋菇亦切小丁備用。

2 鍋熱入油2大匙燒熱，入 **2** 料炒香，續入雞肉炒至肉變白，再入筍、白果、洋菇及 **3** 料煮開，改小火煮至入味，最後入青豆仁及 **4** 料勾芡盛起。

3 麵條置於盤上，淋上 **2** 項之材料拌勻即可。

880g.(2lb.) --- boiled plain noodle
300g.(10½oz.) ---- chicken breast
120g.(4¼oz.) ---- bamboo shoot

100g.(3½oz.) ------- boiled ginkgo nut
50g.(1¾oz.)each --- boiled mushroom, boiled green peas

1
- 2t.each cooking wine, oil
- 1t.corn starch
- ½t.salt
- ¼t.pepper

3
- 2C.stock
- 2t.cooking wine
- 1t.sugar
- ½t.each salt, pepper

2
- 1⅓T.sweet soy bean paste
- 2t.each soy bean paste, hot soy bean paste

4
- 1⅓T.water
- 2t.corn starch

1 Dice chicken into 1 cm square cubes, marinate with **1**. Dice both mushroom and bamboo the same.

2 Heat the wok, add 2T. oil and heat to hot; stri fry **2** until fragrant. Add in chicken, stir fry until color pales. Then stir in bamboo, ginkgo nut, mushroom, and **3**, bring to boil and simmer over low heat until tasty. Add in green peas and thicken with **4**. Remove.

3 Place noodle on a plate, pour over **2** and mix well before serving.

生菜肉醬麵 • *Lettuce and Pork Sauce Noodle*

熟陽春麵 ----------- 880公克	熟筍、新鮮香菇 -各　80公克	
絞肉 ----------------- 240公克	蔥末 --------------------- 1½大匙	
銀芽、生菜 ------各160公克	蒜末 --------------------- 1¼大匙	

❶
- 高湯 ----------------- 1⅓杯
- 醬油 ----------------- 3大匙
- 甜麵醬、酒 ----- 各2大匙
- 麻油 ----------------- 1⅓大匙
- 糖 ----------------- 1大匙
- 胡椒粉、鹽 ------ 各¼小匙

❷ 太白粉、水 ------各1⅓大匙

1 銀芽入開水川燙，生菜洗淨切絲，筍、香菇切小丁備用。
2 鍋熱入油4大匙燒熱，入蔥、蒜末炒香，再入絞肉炒熟，隨入筍、香菇及 ❶ 料煮開，並以 ❷ 料芶芡即為肉醬。
3 麵條置於盤上，上置銀芽、生菜，再淋上肉醬即可。

880g.(2lb.) ---boiled plain noodle
240g.(8²/₅oz.) ------minced pork
160g.(5³/₅oz.)each ---bean sprout, lettuce
80g.(2⁴/₅oz.)each - canned bamboo shoot, fresh black mushroom
1½T. minced green onion
1¼T. ---------minced garlic

❶
- 1⅓C.stock
- 3T.soy sauce
- 2T.each sweet soy bean paste, cooking wine
- 1⅓T.sesame oil
- 1T.sugar
- ¼t.each salt, pepper

❷
- 1⅓T.each corn starch, water

1 Parboil bean sprout; wash lettuce clean and shred. Dice bamboo and mushroom.
2 Heat the wok, add 4T. oil and heat to hot; stir fry green onion and garlic until fragrant. Stir in pork, fry until cooked; add in bamboo, mushroom, and ❶, bring to boil. Thicken with ❷ to be the meat sauce.
3 Place noodle on a plate, arrange bean sprout and lettuce on top. Pour meat sauce over and serve.

臘腸撈麵 • *Sausage Lou Mein*

熟雞蛋麵 ----------- ８８０公克	廣式香腸、肝腸 --------- 各２條
芥藍菜 -------------- ２５０公克	

1 ┌ 高湯 -------------------- 1 杯
│ 蠔油 -------------------- 3 大匙
│ 油 --------------------- 2 大匙
│ 麻油 ------------------ 1⅓大匙
│ 糖 --------------------- 1 小匙
└ 鹽、味精 -------- 各½小匙

2 ┌ 水 ------------------- 1⅓大匙
└ 太白粉 ------------- 2 小匙

1 芥藍菜洗淨，去老纖維，切段，燙熟備用。
2 廣式香腸及肝腸洗淨，入鍋蒸１５分鐘，待涼切斜片，蒸汁留作調味用。
3 **1** 料加蒸汁，入鍋煮開，續入芥藍菜，並以 **2** 料芶芡即為臘腸麵汁。
4 麵條置於盤上，上置臘腸並淋上臘腸麵汁拌勻即可。

880g.(2lb.) ----boiled egg noodle
250g.(8⁴/₅oz.) -------gailan
2 each ----------cantonese sausage, liver sausage

1 ┌ •1C.stock
│ •3T.oyster sauce
│ •2T.oil
│ •1⅓T.sesame oil
│ •1t.sugar
└ •½t.salt

2 ┌ •1⅓T.water
└ •2t.corn starch

1 Wash gailan clean, discard tough fibers; cut into serving sections. Boil until cooked and drain.
2 Wash sausages clean, steam for 15 minutes. When cool, cut into slanting slices, keep the juice for seasoning.
3 Mix the juice with **1** and bring to boil, add in gailan. Thicken with **2** to be the sauce.
4 Place noodle on a plate, arrange sausage slices on top. Pour sauce over and mix well before serving.

豉汁排骨拌麵 · *Pork Rib in Black Bean Sauce Noodle*

熟陽春麵 ----------- 880公克	青椒 ----------------- 240公克	
排骨 ---------------- 300公克	豆豉 ----------------------- 2大匙	

1 〔蔥末、薑末、蒜末 --------
　　-------------- 各1⅓大匙
　　紅辣椒末 ---------- 2小匙〕

3 〔水 ----------------- 1⅓大匙
　　太白粉 ------------- 2小匙〕

2 〔高湯 --------------------- 2杯
　　醬油 ----------------- 2大匙
　　糖 ------------------- 1大匙
　　麻油 ----------------- 2小匙
　　味精 ------------------ ½小匙
　　胡椒粉 -------------- ¼小匙〕

880g.(2lb.) --- boiled plain noodle
300g.(10½oz.) ---- pork rib
240g.(8²/₅oz.) -------- green pepper
2T. ------- fermented black soy bean

1 • 1⅓T. each minced green onion, minced ginger, minced garlic
• 2t. minced red pepper

2 • 2C. stock
• 2T. soy sauce
• 1T. sugar
• 2t. sesame oil
• ¼t. pepper

3 • 1⅓T. water
• 2t. corn starch

1 青椒洗淨切1‧5×2公分小片，入沸水川燙，撈起漂涼，豆豉洗淨切碎備用。

2 鍋熱入油3杯燒至七分熱（160℃），入排骨炸熟取出，鍋內留油2大匙燒熱，入豆豉及 **1** 料爆香，再入 **2** 料及排骨煮開，並以 **3** 料芶芡，再加青椒拌勻即為豉汁排骨。

3 麵條置於盤上，淋上豉汁排骨拌勻即可。

■ 豉汁排骨撈麵：將熟陽春麵改為熟雞蛋麵，其餘材料及做法同豉汁排骨拌麵。

1 Wash green pepper clean, cut into 1.5 x 2 cm pieces; parboil in boiling water, drain and rinsed under cold water. Chop black soy bean.

2 Heat the wok, add 3C. oil and heat to 160℃ (320°F); fry pork rib until cooked, lift out. Keep 2T. oil in the wok and heat to hot, stir fry black soy bean and **1** until fragrant. Add in **2** and pork rib, bring to boil; thicken with **3**, mix in green pepper to be the sauce.

3 Place noodle on a plate, pour over the sauce and mix well before serving.

■ Pork Rib in Black Bean Sauce Lou Mein : Replace boiled plain noodle with boiled egg noodle. The rest of materials and methods are the same as above.

豉汁雞撈麵 · *Chicken in Black Bean Sauce Lou Mein*

熟雞蛋麵 ------------ 880公克	洋蔥末 ---------------------- 3/4杯
雞腿 ----------------- 360公克	豆豉 ----------------- 2大匙
青椒丁 ------------- 140公克	蒜末 ----------------- 2小匙

1 ┌ 醬油、酒 -------- 各2小匙
　　└ 太白粉 ------------- 1小匙

2 ┌ 高湯 ------------------ 1 1/2杯
　　│ 醬油 ------------- 1 1/3大匙
　　│ 太白粉 ------------- 2小匙
　　└ 味精、麻油 ----- 各1/2小匙

1 雞腿洗淨剁2・5×4公分塊狀，入 **1** 料略醃，豆豉洗淨剁碎備用。

2 鍋熱入油3杯燒至七分熱（160℃），入雞塊炸至金黃色撈起。

3 鍋內留油4大匙燒熱，爆香洋蔥，隨入豆豉、蒜末略炒，再入 **2** 料及雞塊煮至黏稠狀，最後灑上青椒丁拌勻即為豆豉雞。

4 麵條置於盤上，淋上豆豉雞拌勻即可。

■ 豉汁雞拌麵：將熟雞蛋麵改為熟陽春麵，其餘材料及做法同豉汁雞撈麵。

880g.(2lb.) ----boiled egg noodle
360g.(12^{7}/$_{10}$oz.) ---chicken leg
140g.(5oz.) --diced green pepper
3/4C. ---------minced onion
2T. -------fermented black soy bean
2t. ----------minced garlic

1 ┌ •2t.each soy sauce, cooking wine
　　└ •1t.corn starch

2 ┌ •1 1/2C.stock
　　│ •1 1/3T.soy sauce
　　│ •2t.corn starch
　　└ •1/2t.sesame oil

1 Wash chicken leg clean and cut into 2.5 x 4 cm serving pieces; marinate in **1** for a while. Rinse black soy bean clean, drain and chop fine.

2 Heat the wok, add 3C. oil and heat to 160℃ (320°F); fry chicken pieces until golden.

3 Keep 4T. oil in the wok and heat to hot, stir fry black soy bean and garlic; add in **2** and chicken, cook until slightly thickened. Mix in green pepper to be the sauce.

4 Place noodle on a plate, pour sauce over and serve.

■ Chicken in Black Bean Sauce Noodle : Replace boiled egg noodle with boiled plain noodle. The rest of materials and methods are the same as above.

蠔油芥菜拌麵 • *Mustard Green and Oyster Sauce Noodle*

熟陽春麵 ----------- 880公克
蔥段 ----------------- 10段

太白粉、水 ----------- 各1大匙

1
┌ 芥菜梗 ------- 400公克
│ 熟筍片 ------- 130公克
│ 熟洋菇片、熟草菇片 -----
└　　　　　----- 各80公克

2
┌ 高湯 ------------- 1½杯
│ 蠔油 ------------- 2大匙
│ 醬油 ------------- 2小匙
└ 糖、鹽、味精 --- 各½小匙

1 芥菜梗切段，入開水燙熟漂涼瀝乾，鍋熱入油4大匙燒熱，入蔥
段爆香，續入 **2** 料煮開，再入 **1** 料並以太白粉水芶芡即為拌料。
2 麵條置於盤上，拌料淋於麵上拌勻即可。

880g.(2lb.) ---boiled plain noodle

10 sections --green onion
1T.each corn starch, water

1
┌ •400g.(14oz.)mustard
│ 　green stem
│ •130g.(4³/₅oz.)canned
│ 　bamboo shoot slices
│ •80g.(2⁴/₅oz.)each
│ 　canned mushroom
│ 　slices, canned straw
└ 　mushroom slices

2
┌ •1½C.stock
│ •2T.oyster sauce
│ •2t.soy sauce
└ •½t.each sugar, salt

1 Cut mustard green stem into serving sections, parboil in boiling water; rinse under cold water and drain. Heat the wok, add 4T. oil and heat to hot; stir fry green onion sections until fragrant. Then add in **2** and bring to boil; add in all materials in **1** and thicken with corn starch and water to be the mixing sauce.
2 Place noodle on a plate, pour sauce over and mix well before serving.

四人份　**serve 4**

蠔油芥藍撈麵 • *Gailan and Oyster Sauce Lou Mein*

熟雞蛋麵 ----------- 880公克
芥藍菜 ------------- 500公克

1
┌ 水 --------------- 1⅓大匙
└ 太白粉 ----------- 2小匙

2
┌ 高湯 -------------- 1杯
│ 油、蠔油 -------- 各3大匙
│ 麻油 ------------- 1⅓大匙
│ 糖 --------------- 1小匙
└ 鹽 --------------- ½小匙

1 芥藍菜洗淨，去老纖維，切段，燙熟備用。
2 將 **2** 料煮開，入芥藍菜拌勻，並以 **1** 料芶芡即為蠔油芥藍。
3 麵條置於盤上，食前再淋上蠔油芥藍並拌勻即可。
■ 蠔油芥藍拌麵：將熟雞蛋麵改為熟陽春麵，其餘材料及做法同蠔
油芥藍撈麵。

880g.(2lb.) ----boiled egg noodle
500g.(17²/₃oz.) ------gailan

1
┌ •1⅓T.water
└ •2t.corn starch

2
┌ •1C.stock
│ •3T.each oil, oyster
│ 　sauce
│ •1⅓T.sesame oil
│ •1t.sugar
└ •½t.salt

1 Wash gailan clean, discard tough fibers; cut into serving sections. Boil until cooked, and drain.
2 Bring **2** to boil, mix well with gailan; thicken with **1** to be noodle sauce.
3 Place noodle on a plate, pour sauce over and mix well before serving.
■ Gailan and Oyster Sauce Noodle : Replace boiled egg noodle with boiled plain noodle. The rest of materials and methods are the same as above.

四人份　**serve 4**

四人份　**serve 4**

海鮮涼麵 · *Seafood Cold Noodle*

熟陽春麵 ----------- ８８０公克　薑片 ---------------- 3 片
蔥段 ---------------------- 5 段

1
　花枝淨重 ----- １００公克
　蝦仁 ----------- ８０公克
　小黃瓜 --------- ７０公克
　海參淨重 ------- ６０公克
　西洋芹 --------- ５０公克
　香菇 ------------- 6 公克

2
　醬油 ---------------- 4 大匙
　芥末醬 ------------- 3 大匙
　白醋 ---------------- 2 大匙
　糖、麻油 ------- 各 1 大匙
　鹽 ------------------ ½ 小匙

1 蝦仁去腸泥洗淨，花枝切花與海參均切片，三者均入沸水中加蔥、薑燙熟。

2 小黃瓜切薄片，西洋芹去老纖維切薄片，香菇泡軟去蒂切片，兩者均入水中燙熟備用。

3 麵條置於盤上，上置 **1** 料，食時再淋上 **2** 料拌勻即可。

880g.(2lb.) --- boiled plain noodle 　 5 sections ---- green onion
　 3 slices -------------- ginger

1
- 100g.(3½oz.) squid (net weight)
- 80g.(2⁴/₅oz.) shelled shrimp
- 70g.(2½oz.) baby cucumber
- 60g.(2¹/₉oz.) sea cucumber (net weight)
- 50g.(1¾oz.) celery
- 6g.(¹/₅oz.) dried black mushroom

2
- 4T.soy sauce
- 3T.mustard
- 2T.white vinegar
- 1T.each sugar, sesame oil
- ½t.salt

1 Devein shrimp and wash clean. Cut squid and sea cucumber into serving pieces or slices. Drop all three into boiling water with green onion and ginger, boil until cooked.

2 Slice cucumber thin; discard tough fibers on celery and slice thin. Soften black mushroom in warm water, discard stem, and slice. Boil celery and mushroom in boiling water until cooked.

3 Place noodle on a plate, arrange all materials of **1** on top. Pour **2** over and mix well before serving.

五彩涼麵 · *Five-Colored Cold Noodle*

熟日式素麵 -------- ８８０公克　　紫菜 ------------------------ 1 張

1
蝦仁 ----------- ２２０公克
小黃瓜 -------- １７０公克
魚板 -------------- ６０公克
蛋 -------------------- 2 個

2
煮出汁 ----------------- 1 杯
味醂、淡色醬油各 4 大匙
柴魚片 -------------- 5 公克

3
蔥末 ----------------- 5 大匙
薑泥 ----------------- 1½大匙

1 蝦仁去腸泥洗淨，入開水燙熟，蛋煎成蛋皮並與小黃瓜、魚板均切絲備用。

2 將 **2** 料煮開過濾即為麵汁。

3 素麵置於盤上，上置 **1** 料，紫菜剪成細絲，灑在上面，食時將 **3** 料加入麵汁中拌勻，取麵沾汁即可。

880g.(2lb.)boiled Japanese So Mein(thin wheat noodle)　　1 sheet ---- dried seaweed

1
- •220g.(7¾oz.) shelled shrimp
- •170g.(6oz.) baby cucumber
- •60g.(2⅑oz.) kamaboko (fish paste block)
- •2 eggs

2
- •1C.seaweed stock
- •4T.each mirin, light brown soy sauce
- •5g.(⅕oz.) dried fish flake

3
- •5T.minced green onion
- •1½T.ginger paste

1 Devein shrimp and wash clean, drop into boiling water until cooked. Beat eggs and make egg crepes, shred. Shred cucumber and kamaboko.

2 Bring **2** to boil and sieve to be the sauce.

3 Place noodle on a plate, arrange all materials of **1** neatly on noodle. Snip seaweed into fine shreds and sprinkle over noodle. Mix **3** with the sauce, dip noodle into the sauce while eating.

牛筋涼麵 · *Beef Tendon Noodle*

熟陽春麵 ------------ 880公克	蔥絲、胡蘿蔔絲 --- 各80公克
熟牛筋 -------------- 300公克	蒜末、香菜末 -------- 各2大匙

1
- 醬油 ---------------- 4大匙
- 麻油、辣油 ------ 各2大匙
- 糖、白醋 -------- 各1大匙

1 熟牛筋切薄片與 **1** 料拌勻略醃使之入味。

2 麵條置於盤上，上置蔥絲、胡蘿蔔絲、蒜末、香菜末，再淋上 **1** 項之材料拌勻即可。

880g.(2lb.) --- boiled plain noodle
300g.(10½oz.) ------ boiled beef tendon
80g.(2⅘oz.) each ---------- shredded carrot, shredded green onion
2T.each ---- minced garlic, minced coriander

1
- 4T.soy sauce
- 2T.each sesame oil, chili oil
- 1T.each sugar, white vinegar

1 Slice beef tendon thin and marinate with **1** for taste.

2 Place noodle on a plate, arrange green onion, carrot, garlic, and coriander on top. Pour **1** over and mix well before serving.

四人份　**serve 4**

四彩涼麵 · *Four-Colored Cold Noodle*

涼

熟陽春麵 ------------ 880公克	蛋 ---------------------------- 2個

1
- 小黃瓜、胡蘿蔔、叉燒肉 ------------------ 各75公克

2
- 冷高湯 -------------- 4大匙
- 芝麻醬、醬油 各2⅔大匙
- 檸檬汁 -------------- 2大匙
- 糖、薑汁 -------- 各1大匙
- 蒜泥、麻油 ------ 各2小匙

1 蛋打散煎成蛋皮，與 **1** 料切絲，置於麵條上。

2 **2** 料拌勻，食時淋於麵條上拌勻即可。

880g.(2lb.) --- boiled plain noodle
2 ------------------------ eggs

1
- 75g.(2⅔oz.)each baby cucumber, Bar-B-Q pork, carrot

2
- 4T.cold stock
- 2⅔T.each sesame paste, soy sauce
- 2T.lemon juice
- 1T.each sugar, ginger juice
- 2t.each garlic paste, sesame oil

1 Beat eggs and make egg crepes, shred. Shred all materials of **1**. Arrange all shreds on top of noodle.

2 Mix **2** evenly, pour over noodle before serving.

　四人份　**serve 4**

翡翠涼麵 • *Green Jade Noodle*

熟菠菜麵 ----------- ８８０公克	紫菜 ------------------------ 1 張
1 ┌ 煮出汁 ------------------ 1杯 　味醂、淡色醬油各４大匙 　柴魚片 ------------ 5公克	**2** ┌ 蔥末、白蘿蔔泥 ---各½杯 　└ 山葵醬 ------------- 2小匙

1 將 **1** 料煮開過濾即為麵汁。
2 麵條置於盤上,紫菜剪成細絲灑在麵上,食時將 **2** 料加入麵汁中拌勻,取麵沾汁即可。
■ 翡翠涼麵之熟菠菜麵可以熟蕎麥麵取代。

880g.(2lb.) ---------- boiled spinach noodle　　1 sheet ----dried seaweed

1 ┌ •1C.seaweed stock
　│ •4T.each mirin, light brown soy sauce
　└ •5g.(⅕oz.) dried fish flake

2 ┌ •½C.each minced green onion, turnip paste
　└ •2t.wasabi (green mustard)

1 Bring **1** to boil and sieve to be clear noodle sauce.
2 Place noodle on a plate, snip seaweed into fine shreds and sprinkle over noodle. Mix **2** well into noodle sauce, dip noodle into sauce during eating.
■ Boiled spinach noodle can be replaced by boiled buckwheat noodle.

四人份　**serve 4**

棒棒雞麵 • *Bon Bon Chicken Noodle*

熟陽春麵 ----------- ８８０公克 蔥末 -------------------- 2 ½大匙	薑末、芝麻醬 ---------- 各½大匙
1 ┌ 雞胸肉 -------- ２００公克 　│ 小黃瓜絲 ----- １５０公克 　└ 海哲皮 -------- １００公克	**2** ┌ 醬油 ----------------- 3大匙 　│ 芝麻醬、糖、白醋 ------- 　│ ---------------------- 各1大匙 　└ 麻油 ----------------- ½大匙

1 雞胸肉煮熟剝絲,海哲皮切絲處理後,加芝麻醬拌勻備用。
2 麵條置於盤上,上置 **1** 料,再灑上蔥、薑末,食時淋上 **2** 料拌勻即可。

880g.(2lb.) ---boiled plain noodle
2½T. minced green onion　　½T. each --minced ginger, sesame paste

1 ┌ •200g.(7oz.)chicken breast
　│ •150g.(5½oz.) shredded cucumber
　└ •100g.(3½oz.)jelly fish

2 ┌ •3T.soy sauce
　│ •1T.each sesame paste, sugar, white vinegar
　└ •½T.sesame oil

1 Boil chicken until cooked, shred by hand. Shred jelly fish and parboil; rinse and drain. Mix both well with sesame paste.
2 Place noodle on a plate, arrange **1** on top; sprinkle with green onion and ginger. Pour over **2** and mix well before serving.

四人份　**serve 4**

怪味雞涼麵 • *Mix-Flavored Chicken Noodle*

熟陽春麵 ---------- ８８０公克　　青江菜 ------------- ３００公克
雞腿 ---------------- ３４０公克

❶
┌ 醬油 ---------------- 4 大匙
│ 花生醬、辣油、蔥末 -----
│ ------------------- 各 2 大匙
│ 糖、白醋 -------- 各 1 大匙
│ 薑末、蒜末 ------ 各 2 小匙
└ 花椒粉 -------------- ½小匙

1 青江菜洗淨切段，入開水川燙，撈起漂涼，雞腿入開水煮約１５分鐘至熟透撈起，待涼切塊備用。

2 麵條置於盤上，上置雞塊、青江菜，並淋 上 **❶** 料拌勻即可。

880g.(2lb.) ---boiled plain noodle　　340g.(12oz.) -chicken leg
300g.(10½oz.) --bok choy

❶
┌ •4T.soy sauce
│ •2T.each peanut paste, chili oil, minced green onion
│ •1T.each sugar, white vinegar
│ •2t.each minced ginger, minced garlic
└ •½t.Szechwan pepper powder

1 Wash bok choy clean and cut into serving sections; boil until cooked and rinse under cold water, drain. Boil chicken leg in boiling water for about 15 minutes or until thoroughly cooked, lift out; cut into serving pieces when cooled.

2 Place noodle on a plate, arrange chicken pieces and bok choy on top. Pour sauce **❶** over before serving.

四川涼麵 · *Szechwan Style Cold Noodle*

熟陽春麵 ----------- ８８０公克

1
青椒 ---------- ２５０公克
里肌肉 -------- １２０公克
酸菜 ------------ ８０公克
洋火腿 ---------- ４０公克
蛋 --------------- ２個

4
水 ------------------- １大匙
鹽 -------------------¼小匙

5
高湯 ----------------- ４大匙
醬油、白醋 ------各２大匙
麻油 ----------------- １大匙
辣油 ----------------- ２小匙
鹽、味精 ---------各¼小匙

2 醬油、酒 ----------各１大匙

3 醬油、糖、白醋 --各１小匙

1 里肌肉切絲，以**2**料拌醃，蛋打散煎成蛋皮，青椒去籽與酸菜、火腿均切絲。
2 鍋熱入油３大匙燒熱，入里肌肉炒熟取出，續入酸菜炒熟並加**3**料調味取出，再入青椒炒熟並加**4**料調味取出。
3 麵條置於盤上，上置**1**料，食時淋上**5**料拌勻即可。

880g.(2lb.) ---boiled plain noodle

1
•250g.(8⁴/₅oz.) green pepper
•120g.(4¹/₄oz.) pork fillet
•80g.(2⁴/₅oz.) sour mustard
•40g.(1²/₅oz.) virginia ham
•2 eggs

2
•1T.each soy sauce, cooking wine

3
•1t.each soy sauce, sugar, white vinegar

4
•1T.water
•¼t.salt

5
•4T.stock
•2T.each soy sauce, white vinegar
•1T.sesame oil
•2t.chili oil
•¼t.salt

1 Shred pork, marinate with **2**. Beat eggs and make egg crepes, shred. Discard seeds in green pepper, shred with sour mustard and ham.
2 Heat the wok, add 3T. oil and heat to hot; stir fry pork until cooked; remove pork. Stir sour mustard into the wok, fry until cooked, season with **3**; remove sour mustard. Stir green pepper into the wok, fry until cooked, season with **4**; remove.
3 Place noodle on a plate, arrange all materials of **1** on top. Pour **5** over and mix well before serving.

什錦涼麵 • *Mixed Cold Noodle*

熟陽春麵 ------------ ８８０公克

1
　小黃瓜 -------- １５０公克
　花枝 ----------- １２０公克
　海哲皮、叉燒肉、雞胸肉
　---------------各８０公克
　香菇 ------------- ６公克

2
　醬油 ---------------- ２小匙
　糖、白醋 -------- 各１小匙
　麻油 --------------- ½小匙
　味精 --------------- ⅛小匙

3
　醬油 ---------------- ２小匙
　糖、酒 ---------- 各１小匙
　麻油 --------------- ½小匙

4
　高湯 ---------------- ６大匙
　醬油 -------------- ２½大匙
　白醋 ------------- １¼大匙
　辣油 --------------- ⅔大匙
　糖 ----------------- ½大匙
　麻油 ------------- １¼小匙
　鹽、味精 -------- 各⅓小匙

1 海哲皮切絲處理後，加 **2** 料醃拌，香菇泡軟去蒂切絲，加 **3** 料醃拌並入鍋蒸熟。
2 花枝去皮切花再切片，與雞胸肉一同入開水中煮熟備用。
3 雞胸肉、小黃瓜、叉燒肉三者均切絲備用
4 麵條置於盤上，上置 **1** 料，食時淋上 **4** 料拌勻即可。

880g.(2lb.) ---boiled plain noodle

1
　•150g.(5⅓oz.) baby cucumber
　•120g.(4¼oz.) squid
　•80g.(2⅘oz.)each jelly fish, Bar-B-Q pork, chicken breast
　•6g.(⅕oz.) dried black mushroom

2
　•2t.soy sauce
　•1t.each sugar, white vinegar
　•½t.sesame oil

3
　•2t.soy sauce
　•1t.each sugar, cooking wine
　•½t.sesame oil

4
　•6T.stock
　•2½T.soy sauce
　•1¼T.white vinegar
　•⅔T.chili oil
　•½T.sugar
　•1¼t.sesame oil
　•⅓t.salt

1 Shred jelly fish, parboil and rinse under cold water, drain; marinate with **2**. Soften mushroom in warm water, discard stem and shred; marinate with **3** and steam until cooked.
2 Skin squid, score the surface and slice. Boil squid with chicken in boiling water until cooked.
3 Shred chicken, cucumber, and Bar-B-Q pork.
4 Place noodle on a plate, arrange all materials of **1** on top. Pour **4** over and mix well before serving.

紅燒涼麵 • *Pork Soy Sauce Noodle*

熟陽春麵 ----------- ８８０公克	香菇 -------------------- １０公克	
梅花肉 ------------- ３００公克	小黃瓜 -------------------- １條	
銀芽 -------------- １２０公克		

❶
水 ----------------------- ２杯
醬油 --------------------- ½杯
酒 ---------------------- ２大匙
糖 ---------------------- １大匙
蔥段 --------------------- ５段
薑片 --------------------- ３片
八角 --------------------- ⅛顆

❷
麻油、辣油、白醋 --------
--------------------- 各１大匙
糖 ---------------------- ２小匙
味精 -------------------- ½小匙

1 銀芽入開水川燙，小黃瓜切薄片備用。
2 鍋熱入油２大匙燒熱，入梅花肉煎至兩面金黃，香菇泡軟去蒂與梅花肉均入 ❶ 料中煮開，改小火滷約１小時，取出待涼，肉切薄片，香菇切絲。
3 取滷肉汁５大匙，加入 ❷ 料拌勻即為涼拌汁。
4 麵條置於盤上，上置肉片、香菇、小黃瓜、銀芽，食時淋上涼拌汁即可。

880g.(2lb.) --- boiled plain noodle
300g.(10½oz.) -------- pork shoulder
120g.(4¼oz.) bean sprout
10g.(⅓oz.) ----- dried black mushroom
1 ----------- baby cucumber

❶
- 2C.water
- ½C. soy sauce
- 2T.cooking wine
- 1T.sugar
- 5 sections green onion
- 3 slices ginger
- ⅛ star anise

❷
- 1T.each sesame oil, chili oil, white vinegar
- 2t.sugar

1 Parboil bean sprout. Slice cucumber thin.
2 Heat the wok, add 2T. oil and heat to hot; fry pork until golden on both side. Soften mushroom in warm water, discard stem; add into pork and **❶**. Bring it to boil and simmer over low heat for one hour. Lift out to cool. Slice pork thin and shred mushroom.
3 Mix **❷** with 5T. sauce to be the noodle sauce.
4 Place noodle on a plate, arrange pork slices, mushroom, cucumber, and bean sprout on top. Pour noodle sauce over before serve.

More Wei-Chuan Cook Books

純青出版社

劃撥帳號：12106299 地址：台北市松江路125號4樓

電話：(02)2508-4331傳真：(02)2507-4902

Distributor: Wei-Chuan Publishing

1455 Monterey Pass Rd., #110
Monterey Park, CA 91754, U.S.A.
Tel: (323)2613880・2613878
Fax: (323)2613299

家常菜
- 226道菜
- 200頁
- 中文版

嬰幼兒食譜
- 140道菜
- 104頁
- 中文版

營養便當
- 88道菜
- 128頁
- 中英對照

家常100
- 100道菜
- 96頁
- 中英對照

素食
- 84道菜
- 120頁
- 中英對照

健康素
- 76道菜
- 96頁
- 中英對照

微波食譜第一冊
- 62道菜
- 112頁
- 中英對照

微波食譜第二冊
- 76道菜
- 128頁
- 中英對照

Favorite Chinese Dishes
- 100 recipes
- 96 pages
- Chinese/English Bilingual

Vegetarian Cooking
- 84 recipes
- 120 pages
- Chinese/English Bilingual

Simply Vegetarian
- 76 recipes
- 96 pages
- Chinese/English Bilingual

Microwave Cooking Chinese Style
- 62 recipes
- 112 pages
- Chinese/English Bilingual

Microwave Cooking Chinese Style 2
- 76 recipes
- 128 pages
- Chinese/English Bilingual

養生家常菜
- 80道菜
- 96頁
- 中英對照

實用烘焙
- 77道點心
- 96頁
- 中英對照

飲茶食譜
- 73道菜
- 128頁
- 中英對照

健康食譜
- 100道菜
- 120頁
- 中英對照

廣東菜
- 75道菜
- 96頁
- 中英對照

Chinese Home Cooking for Health
- 80 recipes
- 96 pages
- Chinese/English Bilingual

International Baking Delight
- 77 recipes
- 96 pages
- Chinese/English Bilingual

Chinese Dim Sum
- 73 recipes
- 128 pages
- Chinese/English Bilingual

Healthful Cooking
- 100 recipes
- 120 pages
- Chinese/English Bilingual

Chinese Cuisine Cantonese Style
- 75 recipes
- 96 pages
- Chinese/English Bilingual

無油煙食譜
- 46道菜
- 68頁/菊16開
- 中文版

快手菜食譜
- 49道菜
- 68頁/菊16開
- 中文版

美容餐食譜
- 50道菜
- 68頁/菊16開
- 中文版

下午茶食譜
- 40道菜
- 68頁/菊16開
- 中文版

懶人餐食譜
- 31套餐
- 68頁/菊16開
- 中文版

米食-家常篇
- 84道菜
- 96頁
- 中英對照

米食-傳統篇
- 82道菜
- 96頁
- 中英對照

麵食-家常篇
- 91道菜
- 96頁
- 中英對照

養生藥膳
- 73道菜
- 128頁
- 中英對照

美味小菜
- 92道菜
- 96頁
- 中英對照

Rice
Home Cooking
- 84 recipes
- 96 pages
- Chinese/English Bilingual

Rice
Traditional Cooking
- 82 recipes
- 96 pages
- Chinese/English Bilingual

Noodles
Home Cooking
- 91 recipes
- 96 pages
- Chinese/English Bilingual

Chinese Herb
Cooking for Health
- 73 recipes
- 128 pages
- Chinese/English Bilingual

Appetizers
- 92 recipes
- 96 pages
- Chinese/English Bilingual

四川菜
- 115道菜
- 96頁
- 中英對照

上海菜
- 91道菜
- 96頁
- 中英對照

台灣菜
- 73道菜
- 120頁
- 中英對照

庖廚偏方　庖廚錦囊　庖廚樂
- 中文版

Chinese Cuisine
Szechwan Style
- 115 recipes
- 96 pages
- Chinese/English Bilingual

Chinese Cuisine
Shanghai Style
- 91 recipes
- 96 pages
- Chinese/English Bilingual

Chinese Cuisine
Taiwanese Style
- 73 recipes
- 120 pages
- Chinese/English Bilingual

味全家政班

味全家政班創立於民國五十年，經過三十餘年的努力，它不只是國內歷史最悠久的家政研習班，更成爲一所正式學制之外的專門學校。

創立之初，味全家政班以教授中國菜及研習烹飪技術爲主，因教學成果良好，備受各界讚譽，乃於民國五十二年，增闢插花、工藝、美容等各門專科，精湛的師資，教學內容的充實，深獲海內外的肯定與好評。

三十餘年來，先後來班參與研習的學員已近二十萬人次，學員的足跡遍及台灣以外，更有許多國外的團體或個人專程抵台，到味全家政求教，在習得中國菜烹調的精髓後，或返回居住地經營餐飲業，或擔任家政教師，或獲聘爲中國餐廳主廚者大有人在，成就倍受激賞。

近年來，味全家政班亞力研究開發改良中國菜餚，並深入國際間，採集各種精緻、道地美食，除了樹立中華文化「食的精神」外，並將各國烹飪口味去蕪存菁，擷取地方特色。爲了確保這些研究工作更加落實，我們特將這些集合海內外餐飲界與研發單位的精典之作，以縝密的拍攝技巧與專業編輯，出版各式食譜，以做傳承。

薪傳與發揚中國烹飪的藝術，是味全家政班一貫的理念，日後，也將秉持宗旨，永續不輟。

Wei-Chuan Cooking School

Since its establishment in 1961, Wei-Chuan Cooki School has made a continuous commitment towa improving and modernizing the culinary art of cookir and special skills training. As a result, it is the olde and most successful school of its kind in Taiwan.

In the beginning, Wei-Chuan Cooking School w primarily teaching and researching Chinese cookir techniques. However, due to popular demand, tl curriculum was expanded to cover courese in flow arrangements, handcrafts, beauty care, dress makir and many other specialized fields by 1963.

The fact that almost 200,000 students, from Taiwe and other countries all over the world, have matric lated in this school can be directly attributed to the hig quality of the teaching staff and the excellent curric lum provided to the studends. Many of the graduat have become successful restaurant owners and che and in numerous cases, respected teachers.

While Wei-Chuan Cooking School has always be committed to developing and improving Chinese c sine, we have recently extended our efforts towa gathering information and researching recipes fr defferent provinces of China. With the same dedic tion to accuracy and perfection as always, we ha begun to publish these authentic regional gourm recipes for our devoted readers. These new public tions will continue to reflect the fine tradition of qual our public has grown to appreciate and expect.